THE BABY SNOOKS SCRIPTS

By Philip Rapp

THE BABY SNOOKS SCRIPTS

By Philip Rapp

Edited By
Ben Ohmart
With
an Introduction by
John Conte

2003
BearManor Media

The Baby Snooks Scripts

© 2003 by Paul Rapp. All rights reserved.

"Foreword" copyright © 2003 by Ben Ohmart

All rights reserved. No part of this publication may be reproduced, stored in a retrieval system or transmitted in any form by any means electronic, mechanical, photocopying, recording or otherwise, except brief extracts for the purpose of review, without the permission of the publisher and copyright owner.

ISBN — 0-59393-057-7

Cover design by Joel Bogart
Typesetting and layout by John Teehan

Printed in the United States of America

by

BearManor Media
P O Box 71426
Albany, GA 31708

www.bearmanormedia.com

For Laura Wagner
A Conte fan,
and a great cheerleader

Table of Contents

Editor's Foreword 1
Introduction 3

April 22, 1939 – Maxwell House Coffee Time 7
January 19, 1939 – Good News of 1939 29
June 18, 1942 – Post Toasties Time 51
January 5, 1939 – Good News of 1939 71
July 3, 1941 – Maxwell House Coffee Time 93
May 5, 1938 – Good News of 1938 111
June 26, 1941 – Maxwell House Coffee Time 141
January 7, 1943 – Maxwell House Coffee Time 157
April 2, 1942 – Maxwell House Coffee Time 173
March 19, 1939 – Screen Guild Show 193

Editor's Foreword

Baby Snooks, with the possible exception of Red Skelton's mean widdle kid, was the champion brat of radio. She was forever asking questions about anything and everything her Daddy was foolish enough to attempt around the house. Her "Why?"s were endless, and often it is difficult to tell if she kept asking because she really cared or just wanted to infuriate her unhappy father. By her giggles, the latter was probably truest.

Fanny Brice was so ingrained into the character of Snooks that it's impossible to imagine anyone else doing the role. Writer Phil Rapp himself would always acknowledge not SNOOKS but BRICE in character names and descriptions of action. Her playful girlie voice held the perfect pitch of awe, shucks and devilment to the tiny antagonist.

But the unsung hero of the story is usually Hanley Stafford as Daddy. Though he wasn't the first actor to play the part, he is without a doubt the most remembered, and the most skilled. His articulation, condescension, exasperation and utter futility of fatherhood made him the perfect foil to the feminine question machine. He had most of the lines and at least half the gags in every script, yet he never commanded the starring credit nor salary to which Ms. Brice aspired. But without his clever and honest acting, it's difficult to say if Baby Snooks would have lasted as long as it did. And does.

It's obvious that Daddy had no idea how to bring up children. He wasted words on Snooks that even bright 40-year-old listeners would have a hard time deciphering. It would've hurt the comedy, but would've helped Snooks' demeanor if Daddy had ignored her questions and said "No!" more often. But there was something about that catalyst Daddy that could never leave well enough alone. Obviously, Snooks was a chump off the ol' block.

Phil Rapp was one of radio's brightest comedy crafters, having written for Eddie Cantor earlier on and creating the Bickersons after he left Fanny Brice's employ. He went on to write some of Danny Kaye's more famous films (*The Life of Walter Mitty, Wonder Man*), and wrote extensively for radio (*The Old Gold Show*) and television (*Topper, Startime, Hiram Holiday*).

As I did with *The Bickersons Scripts*, the 10 radio scripts in this book keep to the format of the original *Good News, Maxwell House Coffee Time*, etc. scripts as close as possible, in order to give radio and history buffs both a true sense of exactly what the actors read. You may find little use for all the coffee commercials, and may wonder why Frank Morgan lies so much throughout a book called *The Baby Snooks Scripts*, but for the sake of completists, of which I am one, I wanted the context as well as the gags to thrive here.

If you like what you read, please get in touch. I have enough material to put out at least 20 more Snooks script books. Rapp reused a lot of his Bickersons material when it was picked up for a new series, but there is more Snooks stuff than can be dreamt of in heaven and earth. Please don't ask "Why?"

– Ben Ohmart
July 2003

Introduction

It was a tremendous experience being MC and singer on *Maxwell House Coffee Time*. That series was always in the top five of popular shows. And then the war came. One week I was making a big (in those days) pot of money, and the next week I was in Uncle Sam's army making $39 a month.

But those four years on *Maxwell House* were some of the best years of my life. Frank Morgan was my mentor, so it was an honor to work as his straight man for the first half of the program, listening to this Baron Munchasen character always trying to top everyone who ever came near him, even himself. The second half of this half-hour series was handled by Fanny Brice as Baby Snooks. She had a wonderful actor on there named Hanley Stafford who played Daddy, whom I would call the centerpiece of the sketch. Baby Snooks' motive each week was to outwit her daddy or drive him to distraction or both. And except for the usual spanking at the end, she *did* both.

Fanny was a tremendous star and a true professional. The remarkable thing to me was, here was this grown woman who had the amazing facility in her throat to make her voice sound like a young girl.

But it was Frank Morgan I spent the most time with. In those days, before the time of audio tape, we had to do two live performances. The first was at 5 in the afternoon from Hollywood that aired at 8 o'clock prime time in New York. When that was over we disbanded for two and a half hours during which time we all had a little bite of dinner and would reconvene to do the live 8 o'clock broadcast for the pacific coast.

Frank was known for his love of the bottle, so the sponsors had given me the responsibility of keeping Frank sober during that interim period. It was delightful fun, because Frank knew what he was doing and would only go so far. But every once in a while he would slip... And the requirements for his performance and the character he played were such that he had to be silver-tongued. His alliteration had to be impeccable, and our writer Phil Rapp wrote a lot of crazy words for him. Monosalavic words that all went into Frank's hyperbole, as he bragged about his exploits each week. My on-air job was to pull him up short and make him face reality. We would dine together almost every week. In that period we'd always go to the Brown Derby which was just a block away on Vine Street in Hollywood, and Frank would promise he wouldn't have more than one cocktail before dinner. At one point, several months into the relationship, we sat down in the restaurant and the waiter took our order (Frank would always have an Old Fashioned, that was his favorite drink). This time the waiter brought the drinks. Mine was in my regular glass, but Frank's was in a glass twice the size of mine. I said, "What's going on here?" Frank said, "Well, ya know, John, I promised I'd only have one drink—this is it!"

The cute thing about this man was—aside from being a great person and a wonderful actor—that he *enjoyed* everything he did. When he would break himself up on the rebroadcast (bare in mind it was the 5 o'clock show that the bosses all listened to in New York, when he was squeaky clean), but he had time by 8 o'clock to imbibe a little, have some food and start feeling great. He'd be rolling along with all the dialogue until he'd make one little blip. He'd mispronounce something and he'd start to giggle and laugh. The whole audience would giggle and laugh, and *we'd* be giggling and laughing. That would throw the timing of the comedy right out the window and we had to be able to cope with all that.

But network radio was very serious business, even when you were doing comedy. You showed up the day before to do a first reading of the script, and you came back the next day for the actual broadcast.

Maxwell House was my favorite radio series to work on. Meredith Wilson wrote the theme for it which I would sing when the show came on the air every week and when it went off the air. It was called "You and I." It became #1 on the Hit Parade and lasted quite a while. It was Meredith's first hit.

During *Maxwell House* we'd sit around the conference table at the first reading with Phil at the head. He would make his notes, but he never had to coach anyone on how to read a line. How do you coach Fanny Brice on how to read a line for Baby Snooks? She *was* that person.

We broadcast on Thursday nights. Our first reading would be on Wednesday. So by the time we showed up on Thursday the new scripts had all been mimeographed. In those days we had what we now call censors. These were network people who would sit up in the sponsor's booth and listen to the dress rehearsal and if there were any elements that were offensive to them, they'd demand that they be changed or taken out or modified in some way. Phil being a very brilliant kind of writer was always ready to settle for second best from these guys. By that I mean he would write in an obvious thing that he *knew* they were going to object to, but meanwhile he was writing in something that was *not* so obvious that they were going to let slide, and that's the way he would get his points over.

There was no adlibbing. Radio writers wanted you to read the gems that they created. That's what they were paid to do: write. Also, the time factor was such that you couldn't wander off then get back on track and hope to pick up and carry on with the script and wind up on the same place on the clock. You'd screw up all the timing.

The interesting thing about *Maxwell House* was the diversity of material within the same show. This was all due to the versatility of our writer (and director, I think), Phil Rapp. His best work was juggling those two characters, Frank Morgan and Fanny Brice. He wrote the entire half-hour. Week after week he churned that stuff out. From the very sophisticated comedy of bumbling, literate liar Frank Morgan, to the what you might call smart-ass child comedy of Baby Snooks, the material on our show had class and variety. And it was great being a part of such *fun*.

– John Conte
March 2003

MAXWELL HOUSE COFFEE TIME
APRIL 22, 1943

1. OPENING

2. CAST INTRO...THEME – "WAIT FOR ME, MARY"

3. MORGAN SPOT

4. MIDDLE COMMERCIAL

5. "IT CAN'T BE WRONG"

6. BABY SNOOKS SPOT

7. CLOSING COMMERCIAL

8. THEME...SIGN-OFF

9. HITCH-HIKE

(ON CUE)

BRICE:	Daddy!
STAFF:	What is it, Snooks?
BRICE:	Do you know how to knit a sweater?
STAFF:	I think so. Are you having trouble?
BRICE:	Yeah. I been working on this sweater for three days.
STAFF:	Can't you finish it?
BRICE:	No—it keeps coming out socks.
STAFF:	Socks! You're probably not following the right pattern.
BRICE:	What pattern?
STAFF:	Didn't they give you any instructions with that wool?
BRICE:	Uh-huh.

STAFF:	Did you follow them?
BRICE:	Uh-huh.
STAFF:	Well, what did they tell you to do?
BRICE:	I dunno.
STAFF:	Do you know how to knit at all?
BRICE:	No.
STAFF:	That's fine. You should always inquire how a thing is made before you try it. Who sold you the wool?
BRICE:	The man in the new store on the corner.
STAFF:	Oh, him! You shouldn't buy wool from him.
BRICE:	Why?
STAFF:	He's just a mug.
BRICE:	Yeah, he acts awful goofy, daddy.
STAFF:	I know it. And you'll never be able to make a sweater out of that stuff.
BRICE:	Why?
STAFF:	Because it's a mug's wool who's goofy time.
BRICE:	Ohhh!

(APPLAUSE...THEME)

HARLOW:	Yes, ladies and gentlemen, with a slight substitution of vowels it'll come out Maxwell House Coffee Time. And that means Frank Morgan, the Maxwell House orchestra, conducted by Frank Tours, Hanley Stafford as Daddy, and Fanny Brice in her role as radio's original problem child—the one, the only Baby Snooks. Now here is our singing master of ceremonies, your host for the evening—John Conte!

WAIT FOR ME MARY – CONTE & ORCHESTRA

(APPLAUSE)

CONTE:	Thank you, ladies and gentlemen, and good evening.
TOURS:	Evening, John. Notice anything different about me?
CONTE:	Different? Can't say I do, Frank.

HARLOW:	Well, I can, John.
CONTE:	Hello, Harlow. What's different about Tours this evening?
HARLOW:	He's wearing a new Easter suit. Am I right, Frank?
TOURS:	That's right, Harlow. You've got very sharp eyes.
CONTE:	He certainly has. That suit you're wearing looks exactly the same as the suit you always wear on Thursday, Tours.
TOURS:	It is exactly the same. That is, it's the same design. But it's a brand new one.
CONTE:	Could have fooled me. How did you know it was his Easter suit, Harlow?
HARLOW:	There's a little egg on his left lapel.
CONTE:	Oh, Easter egg.
TOURS:	It isn't an egg at all, Harlow. That stain happens to be from a Welsh rabbit.
HARLOW:	Well, rabbits or eggs, what's the difference? It still makes it an Easter suit. You're wearing a pretty nifty outfit yourself, John.
CONTE:	Just a little rag my tailor threw together in three months.
TOURS:	I must say you wear your clothes well, old boy. That suit is an outstanding example of sartorial sapidity.
HARLOW:	Oh, I've seen sappier outfits than that.
CONTE:	Sapidity has nothing to do with being sappy, Harlow. It refers to taste.
HARLOW:	I know what it means, John. I like your suit very much—think I'll get one on the same order.
TOURS:	Buying some new clothes, Harlow?
HARLOW:	First thing in the morning. If you'd like to come with me, I can show you where to pick up a couple of snappy models.
MORGAN:	(COMING ON) You can? Well, my wife's out of town and maybe the girls will—
CONTE:	Frank!
	(APPLAUSE)
MORGAN:	Hello, lads. Who are these models, Winkpot? Anybody I know?
HARLOW:	Not woman, Frank—clothes.

MORGAN: Oh, women's clothes. A very dull subject.

CONTE: Don't you like clothes on women, Frank?

MORGAN: Oh the contrary, my boy. A well-groomed woman is a thing of joy. But I fear the fashions this year are a trifle revolting. Skirts are too short.

CONTE: How can you say that, Frank? You know you love short skirts, and they're going to be even higher this year.

MORGAN: Well, I'm afraid the OPA will put a ceiling on them. But it's the colors that bother me. I understand the predominant colors will be pink and green. Hideous combination.

TOURS: Yes, my wife has one.

CONTE: A pink and green dress?

TOURS: No, a hideous combination. Good thing she wears it underneath.

MORGAN: Yes. Still, I think it's decidedly impolitic to bandy your wife's underthings about, Tours. It's amazing what trouble you can get into through one little slip.

CONTE: Yes. Let's steer clear of women's clothes, Frank. What's the newest thing in men's clothes?

MORGAN: Women. We're not steering very well, are we?

HARLOW: Oh, I don't think there's anything wrong with talking about women's clothes. Women do it all the time.

MORGAN: Oh, they do.

HARLOW: You saw my wife's new Easter dress, Frank. Don't you remember we met you at the Derby?

MORGAN: Oh, yes. Wasn't she the lady in the checked dress?

HARLOW: No, she wore it. That blue crepe outfit with streamers.

MORGAN: Err—steamed crabs. Oh, I remember! Very provocative, in an irritating sort of way. I don't think she should have worn a bustle, though.

HARLOW: Bustle? She wasn't wearing any bustle.

MORGAN: Chunky little dickens, isn't she?

CONTE: Now, wait a second, Frank—you've got no right to make disparaging remarks about Mrs. Wilcox's appearance.

HARLOW: Why not?

CONTE: Oh.

MORGAN: That'll hold you for a while, Jockey. As a matter of fact, Winkpot, your wife is a very beautiful girl, and she dresses in extremely fine taste.

HARLOW: Can I tell her you liked her new dress?

MORGAN: I can't see what harm it'll do. Of course, I do think she should cut the guimpe a little lower—sort of emphasize the jabot—then get rid of the flouncing at the bottom and gather it with a nice cross-basting stitch around her peplum.

CONTE: Frank! Why don't you stop that insane talk?

MORGAN: Jockey, you're interrupting the flow of ideas between a coutourier and his client! What time can she come for a fitting, Winkpot?

CONTE: What fitting, Morgan? You don't know a box coat from a cartridge pleat!

MORGAN: Nonsense! Can you name another person who designed skirts for the crowned heads of Europe?

CONTE: They wear skirts on their heads?

MORGAN: Keeps the sun out of their eyes. Who started the sweater fad? Morgan! Who introduced the V-neck, the tea-gown, the U-boat and the Susie Q? (What's that got to do with dresses?)

CONTE: Nothing! And if you insist you're the world's leading stylist, you'll get in trouble.

MORGAN: Why?

CONTE: Well, what about Schiaparelli?

MORGAN: I don't care for Italian food—and don't change the subject! In my day I've made more style history than any man alive. I'm responsible for rubber heels, open toes and flat feet!

CONTE: I suppose you know all about fabrics?

MORGAN: Son, you're looking at the world's biggest fabricator! (That's not the word I had in mind.)

CONTE: Well, it'll do till a better one comes along.

HARLOW: How do you figure out the styles, Frank?

MORGAN: Of course, not all of my styles are planned. Some are the products of pure chance.

CONTE: What do you mean?

MORGAN: Well, for instance, several years ago in London my laundress accidentally put too much starch in my cricket shirt. I wore it at Lord's and I instantly created a riot.

CONTE: Stiff?

MORGAN: Well, I was a little plaster—Oh! Stiff! Yes, the cricket shirt was like a board, but it found favor with society in less than twenty-four hours. From that moment on I was deluged with thousands of offers to design new styles.

HARLOW: Well, well!

MORGAN: Yes. Only this morning I was approached by the restaurant association.

CONTE: Restaurant association?

MORGAN: They want a new vogue for paper panties on lamb chops. They also want to confer a title upon me—Frank Morgan, Coutourier to the Stockyards. You see which way the wind is blowing?

CONTE: Frank, how can you stand there and keep making up those fabulous lies?

MORGAN: That's the last straw. I can show you a cable from the Mayfair Tailors in London, begging to know what I'm going to wear in the Easter Parade!

CONTE: Let's see it.

MORGAN: I have it right here in my—here it is! Read that!

CONTE: Dear Poopsie, if you can ditch your wife this weekend—

MORGAN: Wrong thing! Let me have that, Jockey.

CONTE: Okay, Poopsie.

MORGAN: That's a code message from the Intelligence Department. I wish she was a little more intelligent.

CONTE: Well, where's the wire, liar?

MORGAN: Er—wire. Well, I don't seem to have it on my person—buy they asked me for a ten-word description of my daytime Easter costume.

HARLOW: Ten words? Did you cable them, Frank?

MORGAN: Certainly. I said "Silk hat, Ascot tie, white shirt, coat, vest, pants, love—Frank".

CONTE: What'll you wear at night?

MORGAN: A long flannel nightgown.

HARLOW: Is that all?

MORGAN: That covers everything. But I've always been an authority on correct dress for men. It's commonly known that I change my complete wardrobe four times a day.

HARLOW: I don't like to brag, fellows, but there was a time when I used to change my clothes sixteen times a day.

MORGAN: When was that?

HARLOW: When I was eight months old.

MORGAN: Winkpot, I find your nursery anecdotes revolting. Well, I have to run down to the—

CONTE: Just one second, Frank. How did you discover you had a special talent for designing clothes?

MORGAN: Well, in the days when I was a prominent architect, the graceful lines of my buildings aroused so much comment that—

CONTE: Architect! Don't tell us you designed buildings, Morgan!

MORGAN: (LAUGHS) Are you serious, Jockey! For generations the Morgans have been architects, and one of the greatest draughtsmen in the world was my grandfather, Blueprint Morgan.

CONTE: Blueprint Morgan.

MORGAN: His plans and esquisses were masterpieces of perfection, and to this day, if you visit the British Museum, you may see his famous hanging portico and protruding rotunds.

CONTE: I'll make it a point to check on that.

MORGAN: As a child I had architecture drummed into me morning, noon and night. Each afternoon would find me in my nursery, fondling my blocks, tinkering with my Erector, or fiddling with my Tinkertoy. It was only natural that I should immediately start drawing plans as soon as I could hold a pencil.

CONTE: Oh, stop it! Listen, Frank, I'm convinced you know even less about architecture than you do about designing clothes!

MORGAN: That's a bold accusation, Jockey! Have you ever heard of the heard St. Paul's Cathedral in London?

CONTE: Certainly!

MORGAN: Well, I—

CONTE: That was built by Sir Christopher Wren in 1668!

MORGAN: Err—Christopher...Columbus...1492. Yes. Well, when the Louvre was rebuilt, I was—

CONTE: You were not born! It was done in the seventeenth century by Bernani!

MORGAN: Seventeen bananas. Er—do you know anything about architecture, Jockey?

CONTE:	Plenty. I served as an apprentice for two of America's most celebrated draughtsmen, contributed regular articles to the Architects' Journal, and received further training in Gothic and Renaissance design under Wyndham Tarn at M.I.T.
MORGAN:	Oh—windy Tom. Jockey, you're a living testimonial to the tenet that a little learning is a dangerous thing.
CONTE:	Why?
MORGAN:	There's an old Parthenian proverb that goes as follows: "If thou wouldst grow large carrots thou must sow long seeds—And if thou wouldn't raise the bread of knowledge as well, sow long crumbs." Well, so long, crumbs!
CONTE:	Come back here! If you're telling the truth about all this building baloney, prove it!
MORGAN:	Oh, well—all right. I give you my word of honor that what I'm about to tell you is the plain, unvarnished truth.
CONTE:	The unvarnished truth.
MORGAN:	Yes, I never took a formal course in architecture and I never built a dwelling—
HARLOW:	What?
CONTE:	Uh-huh!
MORGAN:	But I did design, plan and construct—
CONTE:	Here comes the varnish, folks!
MORGAN:	Silence! I constructed for the United States Government, no less, the most modern, startling, and impregnable gold vault this country has ever known.
CONTE:	Now, don't tell us you built the vault at Fort Knox where they store the bullion!
HARLOW:	He's talking about gold—not soup!
MORGAN:	Oh dear. No, Poncho, I am not referring to the vault at Fort Knox. The one I built is located in a secret spot, the whereabouts of which I am not at liberty to divulge.
CONTE:	I knew there was a catch to it. What kind of a building is it?
MORGAN:	I'm coming to that! To begin with, the Government insisted on a dome-shaped structure, with walls of solid steel, five feet thick. In order to make sure of its invulnerability, I built it myself—working from the inside and dispensing with all doors and windows.

HARLOW:	No doors or windows?
MORGAN:	Not an opening anywhere. Working inside the pitch-dark dome, I hermetically sealed every single crack, and after it was approved by Washington, I received my check and the Congressional Medal. I was warmly congratulated by the Pres-
CONTE:	Hold it, Frank! You're nailed now, lovey!
MORGAN:	He shook my—what do you mean?
CONTE:	You just said you built this vault with no doors or windows—and you were working on the inside.
MORGAN:	That's right. My feat was appreciated by the—
CONTE:	Frank! If you were inside this solid steel dome, how did you get out of it?
MORGAN:	Er—solid…Get out..Yes. Well, I stood on my head, balanced my feet in the air, and began to whirl like a top.
CONTE:	How did that get you thru the steel walls?
MORGAN:	I got so dizzy I passed out! So long, fellows, I gotta see a man about a dog kennel!
	(MUSIC…APPLAUSE.)
	MIDDLE COMMERCIAL
CONTE:	Y'know, boys, I've been thinking.
TOURS:	Isn't there a comic song about a farmer named Reuben who does some thinking?
CONTE:	Yes—and that farmer ties in with my thoughts too.
WILCOX:	About what, may I ask?
CONTE:	Cackleberries.
TOURS:	Er…cackleberries?
CONTE:	Sure…*eggs!* Hens cackle and lay eggs—and that's the point. That…and Sunday.
TOURS:	(PUZZLED) Maybe I'm dull, but I can't seem to make… (BRIGHTLY)…Oh, *Sunday!* You mean…
	(WOODWINDS: "THE EASTER PARADE"…FIRST FOUR BARS OF CHORUS)
TOURS:	"The Easter Parade"…also long-eared rabbits, colored eggs and such.

(START COMMERCIAL TIME HERE)

    150 words
    50 seconds, plus
    24 seconds music

WILCOX: What memories that tune brings back, Frank…memories mellow as—say, Maxwell House Coffee!

TOURS: I *knew* you'd say it. And why not a plug for its *richness*?

(STRINGS: SECOND FOUR BARS…FOUR SECONDS)

TOURS: To say nothing of Maxwell House Coffee's *full body*…

(RHYTHM: THIRD FOUR BARS…FOUR SECONDS)

TOURS: …and its vigorous, winy flavor…

(BRASSES: FOURTH FOUR BARS…FOUR SECONDS)

WILCOX: Nice line-up of features, Frank. But I always say…

TOURS: I know. When poorly blended…

(ORCHESTRA: FIRST EIGHT BARS RUSHED & SOUR…FOUR SECONDS)

TOURS: …and when skillfully blended…

(ORCHESTRA: LAST EIGHT BARS SWEET…EIGHT SECONDS)

WILCOX: Exactly—and thanks very much for the illustration!

Friends, it takes that same skillful blending of choice Latin-American coffees to produce the mellowness and richness, the full body and vigorous flavor, of Maxwell House. Those outstanding qualities "parade" across the country…reminding millions that here, indeed, is truly good coffee!

And so I remind you, friends—since we can't *buy* all the coffee we'd like, we sure can *like* all we buy. What say we ask for Maxwell House Coffee…now, as always—*Good* to the *Last* Drop!

WILCOX: And now, the voice of John Conte in a Carmen Dragon arrangement of "It Can't Be Wrong." Frank Tours conducting.

"IT CANT' BE WRONG" – CONTE & ORCHESTRA

(APPLAUSE)

CONTE: Thank you, ladies and Gentlemen. And now—

STAFF: Say, John!

CONTE: Yes, daddy?

STAFF:	You remember we had a visit from my Uncle Bushrod several weeks ago?
CONTE:	Oh, yes.
STAFF:	Well, he remembered me in his will.
CONTE:	His will! You mean—
STAFF:	Yes. Poor old gent. I inherited his house in the mountains. I was rather excited because I knew he'd amassed a fortune during his lifetime, so I took Snooks on the train and we went up to see what the place was like. We arrived late at night—(FADES) and the station was the most desolate—

(SNOOKS PLAY-ON)

(SOUND OF TRAIN PULLING AWAY...TRAIN BELL)

FATHER:	Well, here we are, Snooks.
BRICE:	Where are we, daddy?
FATHER:	The name of this station is Bagel Hollow. It's only a whistle stop.
BRICE:	Who's whistling, daddy?
FATHER:	Nobody's whistling. This is just a tiny depot—nothing stops here but milk trains.
BRICE:	Do they milk trains?
FATHER:	Sure. Come on—let's start moving.
BRICE:	Where are we going?
FATHER:	I told you fifty times. We're going to Uncle Bushrod's house.
BRICE:	Is Uncle Bushrod gonna be there?
FATHER:	No. Uncle Bushrod's passed on. He's gone to a better world—I hope.
BRICE:	When is he coming back?
FATHER:	He's never coming back, Snooks. He's left this vale of tears for good.
BRICE:	Shall we cry, daddy?
FATHER:	I don't think it's necessary. He was ninety-two when he died—and he lived a pretty full life.
BRICE:	He wasn't full all the time, was he?
FATHER:	Don't be disrespectful. De mortuis nil nisi bonum.

BRICE: Huh?

FATHER: Nothing. Carry this small bag—and I'll take the portable radio.

BRICE: Yes, daddy…Daddy?

FATHER: What is it?

BRICE: Did Uncle Bushrod leave his shoes?

FATHER: His shoes? I suppose so.

BRICE: Can I see them?

FATHER: What for?

BRICE: 'Cause I heard you tell mummy he was well heeled.

FATHER: That has nothing to do with his shoes. Let's walk a little faster, Snooks. (FADE IN HORSE AND WAGON) It's pretty dark and we still have about a quarter of a mile to go.

BRICE: There's a man with a horse and buggy, daddy!

FATHER: Good. Maybe he'll give us a lift. Signal him for a hitch, Snooks.

BRICE: Shall I do it like in the movies where the girl picks up her—

FATHER: No! Just yell!

BRICE: Hey, mister!

MAN: Whoa, Cherry!

(WAGON STOPS)

FATHER: Can you give us a lift, brother?

MAN: You bet. Climb aboard, brother.

FATHER: Thanks, brother.

BRICE: Is he your brother, daddy?

FATHER: No. Come on, I'll help you get on the wagon. Let me have the bag. All right, now—put your foot in the spoke.

BRICE: What spoke?

FATHER: The wheel spoke.

BRICE: The wheel spoke?

FATHER: Yes.

BRICE: I didn't hear nothing.

FATHER: Oh, step on that wheel! Come on—up! There!

MAN:	Are ye set, sister?
BRICE:	I'm set, brother.
MAN:	Giddyap, Cherry! (WAGON STARTS OFF)
BRICE:	It's awful dark, daddy.
FATHER:	We'll be there in a few minutes.
MAN:	Where by ye headin' fer?
FATHER:	The old Higgins' house.
MAN:	Whoa, Cherry! (WAGON STOPS)…Did ye say the Higgins' house?
FATHER:	That's right.
MAN:	Old Bushrod's place?
FATHER:	Yes.
MAN:	Giddyap, Cherry! (WAGON MOVES ALONG)
BRICE:	What's the matter, daddy?
FATHER:	I don't know. He gave us a very queer look….Say, brother, I'm the—er—the new owner of the house. Bushrod was my uncle.
MAN:	Whoa, Cherry…(WAGON STOPS) Ye say ye own the house?
FATHER:	Yes, my uncle willed it to me.
MAN:	Giddyap! (WAGON MOVES)
BRICE:	He scares me, daddy.
FATHER:	Shh…Er—anything wrong with the house, neighbor?
MAN:	Ain't sayin' there is—ain't saying there sin't.
FATHER:	Oh. Well, there's no train back this evening and we have to spend the night there.
MAN:	Hey?
FATHER:	I say we have to spend the night there.
BRICE:	Whoa, Cherry! (WAGON STOPS)
MAN:	Wouldn't stay there if I was you.
FATHER:	Why not?
MAN:	Ye believe in ghosts?
FATHER:	Nonsense!

MAN:	Giddyap!...(WAGON STARTS) ...Shame to stunt the little girl's growth.
BRICE:	Is there goats there, daddy?
FATHER:	No. He said ghosts.
BRICE:	What's ghosts?
FATHER:	Ghosts are supposed to be supernatural beings—spirit bodies of departed persons. It's a lot of twaddle, isn't it...Isn't it?
BRICE:	Is it?
FATHER:	Certainly. I heard a good joke about ghosts yesterday. Two ghosts were sitting on a bed when suddenly they heard a noise.
BRICE:	(LAUGHS) That's awful funny, daddy.
FATHER:	I'm not finished yet.
BRICE:	Oh.
FATHER:	Suddenly they heard a noise and one ghost turned to the other and said, "Do you believe in people?" (LAUGHS LIKE HELL)
BRICE:	(LAUGHS)
FATHER:	(LAUGHING) Get it?
BRICE:	No.
MAN:	Whoa,....(WAGON STOPS) ...Here's the house.
FATHER:	Oh....Hmm...Bleak looking place, isn't it?...Well—come on, Snooks. Don't forget the radio.
BRICE:	I got it, daddy. (SOUND OF GETTING OFF WAGON)
FATHER:	There we are! Thanks a lot, brother.
MAN:	Shame to stunt the little girl's growth....Giddyap!
	(WAGON MOVES OUT)
FATHER:	Well, let's go in...(KEY IN LOCK...SQUEAKY DOOR OPENS)
BRICE:	Put the lights on, daddy.
FATHER:	Just a second—I'll light a match and find the switch. (LIGHTS IT) Hmmmm...No electricity here.
	(WIND WHISTLES THRU......DOOR SQUEAKS SHUT)
BRICE:	What's that?
FATHER:	Just the wind—blew the door shut. There's a couple of candles on that sideboard. Bring them over here.

BRICE:	I wanna go home!
FATHER:	Now, don't be silly. As soon as I light these candles you'll feel better....There.
BRICE:	Let me hold one.
FATHER:	Okay. We won't be able to see much tonight. Let's find the bedroom and go to sleep....Follow me. (HOLLOW FOOTSTEPS)
BRICE:	Daddy!
FATHER:	What is it?
BRICE:	(EXCITED) Uncle Louie's here!
FATHER:	Where?
BRICE:	In that room!
FATHER:	What are you talking about? Where's Uncle Louie?
BRICE:	There he is—looking thru that hole in the wall.
FATHER:	That's not Uncle Louie—that's a moose-head! Come on let's find the bedroom! This broken-down joint gives me the creeps! Don't let your candle go out.
BRICE:	Why?
FATHER:	Because I haven't got any more matches! Come on.
	(WIND WHISTLES THRU...FOOTSTEPS)
BRICE:	Daddy!
FATHER:	(A LITTLE OFF) What is it?
BRICE:	The wind blew my candle out.
FATHER:	I told you to be—oops! I dropped mine, too! Now we haven't got a light at all! Just stand still a few seconds until your eyes become accustomed to the darkness...(WIND WHISTLES)...Stop poking me in the leg, Snooks!
BRICE:	I'm way over here, Daddy.
FATHER:	Huh?...Oh—it's just the corner of this table. Stand where you are—I'll come and get you. (FOOTSTEPS) Let me feel around a minute....Here's a couch. Lie down—I'll cover you with my coat.
BRICE:	Where are you gonna sleep, Daddy?
FATHER:	I'll rest on the floor. (WIND WHISTLES) Now, try and go right to sleep. Goodnight.

BRICE: Goodnight.
BRICE: (YELLS) Daddy!
FATHER: What is it?
BRICE: My toe hurts.
FATHER: Which toe?
BRICE: The youngest one. It hurts me.
FATHER: What's the matter with it?
BRICE: It hurts every time I pinch it.
FATHER: Well, don't pinch it!
BRICE: Then how can I tell if it hurts?
FATHER: Oh, go to sleep.
BRICE: I'm scared. Put the lights on.
            (WIND WHISTLES)
FATHER: There aren't any lights here—and I have no matches! Just go to sleep. I'm here with you.
BRICE: Put on the radio.
FATHER: No! Go to sleep! Sorry I ever came to this musty joint!
BRICE: Daddy!
FATHER: What do you want?
BRICE: Tell me a story.
FATHER: A story!
BRICE: Yeah—a ghost story.
FATHER: Fine! That would be just the thing for a night like this!
BRICE: Then tell me about Jack and the Beanstalk.
FATHER: Oh, all right—I'll tell it quickly and no interruptions. Once upon a time there was a little boy named Jack. He lived with ———-
BRICE: Jack who?
FATHER: Just Jack! He lived with his mother and they were very poor. But she was always good to him and—
BRICE: Good to who, daddy?
FATHER: Good to Jack! She was—

BRICE:	Who was?
FATHER:	His mother.
BRICE:	Whose mother?
FATHER:	Jack's mother!
BRICE:	Ohhhhh!
FATHER:	Now, don't interrupt any more or I won't finish the story!
BRICE:	Finish it, daddy.
FATHER:	All right! There was something with a cow—then something else and then somehow he got some beans. For the cow, I think.
BRICE:	The cow ate the beans?
FATHER:	No!
BRICE:	The beans ate the cow?
FATHER:	Nobody ate anything!
BRICE:	Why?
FATHER:	Keep quiet!
	(WIND WHISTLES....ERRIE NOISES....SHUTTER SLAMS)
BRICE:	I like it better when we're talking, daddy.
FATHER:	Y-yes. Wish we had a light here. Anyhow, when Jack brought home the beans his mother threw them out of the window and in the morning when Jack woke up—he saw — Snooks.
BRICE:	(QUIETLY) Yes, daddy?
FATHER:	Okay. I just wanted to make sure you were all right.
BRICE:	What did Jack see, daddy?
FATHER:	A great big beanstalk. He climbed up the beanstalk and found himself in a strange land. Pretty soon he came to the castle of a giant and—and—I'll tell you the rest of the story in the morning.
BRICE:	Why?
FATHER:	Because this part about the giant is pretty scarey—it might make you have unpleasant dreams.
BRICE:	Finish the story!
FATHER:	No!
BRICE:	Waaahhhh!

FATHER:	All right—but if you get scared don't blame me! Jack broke into the giant's castle and found himself in a damp, dark, dungeon.
BRICE:	Uh-huh.
FATHER:	(VOICE GETS WEIRD) The place was full of cobwebs and weird little animals and bats.
BRICE:	(LAUGHS) Waaaahh!
FATHER:	You see? You're afraid!
BRICE:	No I ain't. I like it.
FATHER:	Then why did you cry?
BRICE:	I started to laugh but I remembered my toe hurts. Finish it, daddy.
FATHER:	All right…(WIND WHISTLES)….Jack felt around the walls and he was shaking from head to foot….Pretty soon—from out of the blackness—he heard a terrible sound…Thump…Thump…Thump…
	(ON THE SECOND THUMP SOUND PICKS IT UP)
FATHER:	A cold sweat broke out on—(HIS VOICE SHAKES) Snooks.
BRICE:	Huh?
FATHER:	Did you hear anything when I said thump?
BRICE:	No.
FATHER:	Maybe—er—maybe you'd better turn on the radio.
BRICE:	Are you scared, daddy?
FATHER:	No—but we'll be able to listen to some music. It'll be comforting.
BRICE:	Yeah—turn it on.
	(CLICK)
	(TERRIFIC CLASH OF GONG)
VOICE:	(FILTER) This is the Horror Program—featuring the Headless Maniac!
FATHER:	Oh, nuts! (CLICK) G-goodnight, Snooks.
BRICE:	Goodnight, daddy.
	(MUSIC…APPLAUSE)
	CLOSING COMMERCIAL

TOURS: About Easter Sunday again, John…

CONTE: Never mind, Frank…there'll be eggs enough, I suppose.

WILCOX: Have you tried to buy any *chocolate* ones?

TOURS: What I wish to say about Easter has nothing whatever to do with eggs—chicken *or* chocolate.

CONTE: Then what's on your mind, Frank?

WILCOX: Maybe he recalls that *Christmas* was four months ago.

TOURS: So it was! But *April* twenty-fifth is a date that *you*, Harlow, should remember.

(STAFF COMMERCIAL TIME HERE)

182 words
1 min. 3 sec.

WILCOX: Sure enough…it's the day the current coffee ration period ends. So friends—if you've been holding out stamp twenty-six to use to buy coffee this weekend, why not get truly *good* coffee? That's Maxwell House…and for good *reasons*!

One is the *skillful* blending that has distinguished Maxwell House Coffee for more than half a century…blending that accounts for the deep-down coffee satisfaction in every cup you drink.

Another reason Maxwell House Coffee provides so much pleasure is "Radiant Roast"…the famous process specially designed to bring out the *full* flavor, fragrance and strength of every Latin-American bean. But *buying* good coffee and *brewing* good coffee are two different things. That's why directions covering the various coffee-making methods are printed on the Maxwell House label. Follow them to the *letter* and you'll make coffee *better*…and economically, too!

Come Monday, ladies, a new ration period begins. And you can use stamp number twenty-three to buy a pound of coffee. And since you'll want a pound of truly *good* coffee, ask your grocer for…*Maxwell House*!

(THEME)

(EASTERN BROADCAST ONLY)

MUSIC: THEME…FADES FOR:

CONTE: Which rings down the curtain for tonight, ladies and gentlemen, until next Thursday evening at Maxwell House Coffee Time…when we return with Fanny Brice as Baby Snooks, Frank Morgan, who appears with us through the courtesy of Metro-Goldwyn-Mayer and who will next be seen in "The Human Comedy," Hanley Stafford, Frank Tours and Harlow Wilcox.

Maxwell House Coffee Time is written by Phil Rapp.

This is John Conte, saying goodnight and good luck from the makers of Maxwell House. And, friends, now that you're going to drink your coffee down to the last drop, wouldn't it be smart to buy Maxwell House—the coffee that's always—Good to the Last Drop.

(REPEAT SHOW ONLY)

MUSIC: THEME…FADES FOR:

CONTE: Which rings down the curtain for tonight, ladies and gentlemen, until next Thursday evening at Maxwell House Coffee Time…when we return with Fanny Brice as Baby Snooks, Frank Morgan, who appears with us through the courtesy of Metro-Goldwyn-Mayer, and who will next be seen in "The Human Comedy," Hanley Stafford, Frank Tours and Harlow Wilcox.

Maxwell House Coffee Time is written by Phil Rapp.

And say, be sure to listen to Hal Burdick and his famous "Night Editor" stories…fifteen minutes of grand entertainment…presented over many of these stations every Thursday immediately before Maxwell House Coffee Time.

This is John Conte, saying goodnight and good luck from the makers of Maxwell House. And, friends, now that you're going to drink your coffee down to the last drop, wouldn't it be smart to buy Maxwell House—the coffee that's always—Good to the Last Drop.

HITCH-HIKE

ANNOUNCER: She's a *speed* demon!

SOUND: (TYPING AT FAST CLIP…TWO SECONDS)

ANNOUNCER: Her *ten flying fingers* type letters in a flash! And *like* a flash, at breakfast, millions of other fingers "fly" for *Post-Tens*…the single package containing *ten individual* boxes of delicious cereals! Post's Bran Flakes, Post Toasties, Grape Nuts, Grape Nut *Flakes*, Nabisco Shredded Wheat. All supply important whole-grain nourishment ...and they're *not* rationed. So mother, see that those "flying fingers" at *your* breakfast table connect with...*Post-Tens*!

This program came to you from Hollywood.

THIS IS THE NATIONAL BROADCASTING COMPANY.

MAXWELL HOUSE
PRESENTS
"GOOD NEWS OF 1939"
JANUARY 19, 1939
56

CAST

1. Warren Hull
2. Robert Young
3. Virginia Bruce
4. Melvyn Douglas
5. Zarova
6. Tony Martin
7. Frank Morgan
8. Fanny Brice
9. Hanley Stafford
10. Meredith Willson and Orchestra
11. Max Terr Chorus

MAXWELL HOUSE
JANUARY 19, 1939

PAGE 1	OPENING BAND – "HONOLULU"
2 - 2E	YOUNG – DOUGLAS – WILLSON – MARTIN
	MARTIN – "YOU"
3 - 3F	"BABY SNOOKS"
4 - 4A	COMMERCIAL
5	BAND – "HOW STRANGE" – ZAROVA
6 - 6E	MORGAN – YOUNG
7	STATION BREAK
8	BAND – "WHAT HAVE YOU GOT THAT GETS ME"
9 - 9L	"BOHEMIANS" – DOUGLAS – BRUCE
10	MARTIN – "THIS NIGHT WILL BE MY SOUVENIR"

11 - 11A   COMMERCIAL

12 - 12A   DOUGLAS – BRUCE – YOUNG – WILLSON

CONCERT HALL – "MARCHE MILITAIRE"

13 - 13A   CLOSING

HULL: Maxwell Coffee presents...Good News of 1939!

MUSIC: IN AND FADE

HULL: Once again the makers of Maxwell House Coffee welcome you to an hour of entertainment from the Metro-Goldwyn-Mayer studios in Hollywood. Tonight you will hear all of the regular Good News cast, plus two guest stars who are favorites of yours. And here is your host for the evening—Robert Young!

MUSIC: OUT

(APPLAUSE)

YOUNG: Thank you, Warren. For the benefit of any new subscribers to our series, our guests of honor this evening are two young people who were with us two weeks ago—Miss Virginia Bruce and Mr. Melvyn Douglas. Regular subscribers may remember that Melvyn made his last visit the occasion for some critical remarks about radio programs, so tonight I asked him—always the perfect host, that's me—I asked him if he was going to give us another going over. He said no, tonight he planned to deliver a diatribe on what is wrong with motion pictures. Well, that diatribe business had me worried, too - and sure enough I find we're in for it again. According to Frank Morgan, diatribe is a word derived from the Hindu "dia" - meaning double...and the Arabian word treeva, meaning tripe. You can piece the word together yourselves. Now—Meredith Willson's going to start our Maxwell House program in just a moment with the title song from the new picture *Honolulu*. Now—Meredith!

"HONOLULU" – ORCHESTRA

(APPLAUSE)

YOUNG: That was "Honolulu," from the picture *Honolulu*, starring Eleanor Powell, George Burns and Gracie Allen, and your humble servant, Robert Young. I'll let you know when to expect it at your favorite theater.

DOUGLAS: Always the business man, eh Robert? Why don't you mention some of my pictures?

YOUNG: Oh, hello Melvyn! Ladies and gentlemen, this is Melvyn Douglas—(APPLAUSE) and if you haven't already seen it, don't miss *The Shining Hour*, starring Joan Crawford, with Mr. Douglas, and your humble servant Robert Young.

DOUGLAS: You just can't keep the guy out of anything.

YOUNG: No. Maybe that's what Professor Douglas thinks is wrong with pictures.

DOUGLAS: Not at all. Hollywood needs more actors of your stamp. No Bob, I've analyzed the movies very exhaustively, and I have reached the following conclusion!

YOUNG: The diatribe.

DOUGLAS: Yes. The trouble with movies, my boy, is they aren't true enough to life. Ever see a movie in which a fellow meets a girl in some natural, every day way? No. He has never seen the girl until he saves her from drowning!

YOUNG: Well, what's so unlikely about that?

DOUGLAS: Did you ever save a girl from drowning?

YOUNG: No. I've never even *seen* a girl drowning. But you can't go by me. I never even won a raffle!

DOUGLAS: Listen, if you see a girl drowning, that's no guarantee of romance, and I know.

YOUNG: You saw one?

DOUGLAS: Yes. I saw a girl drowning in a lake where I was fishing once.

YOUNG: A perfect opportunity! Did you dive in and save her?

DOUGLAS: No, I paddled over to where she was and pulled her in with a boat hook.

YOUNG: Well, a boat hook isn't as romantic as jumping in, but you saved her life! Was she grateful?

DOUGLAS: I guess so. She made me row her over to where her husband was standing, on the shore, and he gave me a dollar.

YOUNG: Hm. How are you at fires, Mel? Ever meet any girls in buildings?

DOUGLAS: No. Not a spark of romance has Douglas ever picked up from a fire. I'll tell you another one of the difficulties. Even if my luck was better—I don't think I'm ever prepared, psychologically, for the lovely encounter.

MEREDITH: Gee, this is interesting, Mr. Douglas.

DOUGLAS: Oh—thank you.

YOUNG: What Meredith probably means is he doesn't understand what you just said. Give it to him again in easy words, Mel.

DOUGLAS: Well, Meredith, if you've been to many movies, you know that the hero always meets the girl rather suddenly and surprisingly.

MEREDITH: Yes.

DOUGLAS: For instance—He has a drawing room on a train, and the conductor shoves the girl into his room without a word to anybody...Or he's sitting on a bench in a park, and a girl comes along on a runaway horse. But the point is that whatever it is, the hero in a picture is always ready for it, and I'm not. There's just a split second when you have to decide what to do, and that doesn't seem to be enough time for me. I hear the runaway horse in the park—I look up—there it is—I lay down my newspaper—horse is fifty yards past me.

MEREDITH: What about the girl in your drawing room? That sounds good to me.

YOUNG: Meredith! It doesn't sound bad, at that. And what could go wrong?

DOUGLAS: It's no good, Bob. That one happened to me, too. Drawing Room A, Car 54, door opens, conductor says "This is yours, Miss," shuts the door— I turn around—beautiful girl—she screams and runs out.

MEREDITH: What for?

DOUGLAS: Well, I was shaving, and I didn't have any pants on. Never saw her again.

YOUNG: Melvyn, you're just incompetent. I'll bet there are lots of fellows who've had romantic encounters that really worked out. Ask some of the boys on the program. Ask Tony Martin—ask Frank Morgan—

MEREDITH: Ask me, Mr. Douglas!

DOUG: Oh. Well all right, Meredith, I'll ask you. Have you had romantic, unexpected encounters with glamorous ladies—and did they work out?

MEREDITH: Did they! Boy, oh boy!

YOUNG: Now Meredith, control yourself. This is a scientific investigation. Speak up.

MEREDITH: Oh, sure! Well, one day about ten years ago I was in the woods.

DOUGLAS:	Sounds promising.
YOUNG:	What were you doing in the woods, Meredith? Gathering nuts for the winter?
MEREDITH:	Oh no. There was a lot of us there. It was a church social.
YOUNG:	A church social? Strawberry supper?
MEREDITH:	Chicken plate. Well, I was sitting under a big tree enjoying my second helping, and minding my own business, when all of a sudden I heard a beautiful voice say, "Have more chicken, Mister?"
DOUGLAS:	But hark! What voice from yonder window breaks? It is the East, and Juliet is the sun!
MEREDITH:	No, it wasn't Juliet, but it was a mighty pretty girl.
DOUGLAS:	All right—how did you handle the situation? Were you cool?
MEREDITH:	(WITH A SIMPER) Well—not *too* cool! But I handled it fine. She said, "Have some more chicken, Mister?" And I said, "I don't mind if I do."
YOUNG:	How could she resist that?
DOUGLAS:	No woman could. How did you follow it up, Meredith?
MEREDITH:	Well sir, she was just about to go get me the chicken, when up comes a lady I knew, and said, "Meredith, shake hands with Peggy,"…and I did, and pretty soon I got to know her, and I started a whirlwind courtship.
YOUNG:	Fast worker, huh?
MEREDITH:	Yep. I was engaged to her inside of a year, and three years later she led me to the altar, and she now has the honor to be Mrs. Meredith—I mean I now have the honor to be Mrs. Peggy—she's my wife!
DOUGLAS:	Well I've got to admit—romance still lives.
YOUNG:	Did you live happily ever after, Meredith?
MEREDITH:	Oh, she can't complain.
YOUNG:	You see Melvyn, I told you—do you need any more proof?
DOUGLAS:	I think so.
YOUNG:	Must be dozens of cases right here on the program. Let's see— Tony Martin—Tony!
MARTIN:	Yes, Bob? Hello Melvyn.
DOUGLAS:	Hi, Tony.

YOUNG:	We're having an argument about pictures. Would you mind telling us how you first met Alice Faye?
MARTIN:	Not at all. Alice and I first met in a revolving door.
YOUNG:	A revolving door?
MARTIN:	Sure! That's when we started going around together! (LAUGHS)
YOUNG:	Pick up the marbles, Melvyn. Tony, you better sing.
MARTIN:	Okay, I've got a song that'll tear down the house.
DOUGLAS:	Fine! I'll sit down over here— maybe I'll get a chance to rescue somebody.

"YOU" – ORCHESTRA AND MARTIN CLAP

YOUNG:	That was Tony Martin singing, "You," which was introduced by Virginia Bruce in *The Great Ziegfield*.

And now, ladies and gentlemen, here is Fanny Brice as Baby Snooks!

(MUSIC...APPLAUSE)

Tonight, for a reason which he will soon explain, Daddy, played by Hanley Stafford, is going to spend the night in the nursery with Baby Snooks... Praying that he will find her asleep - he quietly sneaks in, very careful not to make a sound...Listen.

(TERRIFIC CRASH)

FATHER:	(ANGRY MUTTER) Ahhh—always leaves things in the middle of the floor. (UNINTELLIGIBLE MUTTER)
BRICE:	Who's that?
FATHER:	I'm sorry, Snooks. Go back to sleep.
BRICE:	I ain't been sleeping, daddy.
FATHER:	What are you talking about? You went to bed at seven o'clock and it's now one. You must have been sleeping.
BRICE:	No, I wasn't.
FATHER:	Well, what were you doing in the interim?
BRICE:	Huh?
FATHER:	I said what were you doing in the interim?
BRICE:	I didn't go there! I stayed in bed all the time!
FATHER:	Well, go to sleep now. I'm going to stay in your room tonight.

BRICE:	Why?
FATHER:	Because—er—because the traffic passes our window and I—er—I can't stand the noise.
BRICE:	Oh…Daddy?
FATHER:	What is it?
BRICE:	Why did mummy chase you out?
FATHER:	YOU MIND YOUR OWN BUSINESS! Now you go to sleep and let me get some rest on the couch.
BRICE:	Sing me to sleep, daddy.
FATHER:	Oh all right (SINGS SOFTLY)…Rockabye baby on the tree top-when the wind blows (YAWNS AND SINGS) the cradle will rock…(YAWNS)…When the bow-breaks…the—cradle will—(DIES OUT WITH A YAWN)…
	(LOUD SNORE)
BRICE:	(YELLS) Daddy!
FATHER:	Huh? What? What is it?
BRICE:	Can I bring the dog up here?
FATHER:	The dog? What do you want the dog for—I'm here!
BRICE:	I want him to sleep with me.
FATHER:	No! You can't put the dog in bed with you!
BRICE:	Why?
FATHER:	Because I won't sleep in the same room with the dog!
BRICE:	Why?
FATHER:	Because it isn't healthy!
BRICE:	Will the dog get sick?
FATHER:	Oh, no! Go to sleep.
BRICE:	Awight…Daddy?
FATHER:	Now, what is it?
BRICE:	If I go to sleep will you buy me a new dolly?
FATHER:	Yes.
BRICE:	When?
FATHER:	(DEAD TIRED) Tomorrow.

BRICE: What kind?

FATHER: Any kind. Go to sleep.

BRICE: Can I have a dolly that says mama?

FATHER: Yes.

BRICE: And with teeth that come out?

FATHER: Teeth that come out?

BRICE: Like Uncle Louie.

FATHER: Listen here, Snooks- you stop making remarks about Uncle Louie- he's a very nice uncle.

BRICE: How did he get to be my uncle, daddy?

FATHER: He's related to you because he's my half brother.

BRICE: Half brother?

FATHER: Yes. I have two half brothers and three half sisters.

BRICE: Are you the only whole one in the family?

FATHER: Will you please stop asking questions and let me get an hour's sleep?

BRICE: Tell me a story.

FATHER: No.

BRICE: Waaaahhh!

FATHER: All right, all right! If you promise not to interrupt, I'll tell you the story of Little Red Riding Hood.

BRICE: I promise, daddy.

FATHER: All right.

BRICE: Put on the light.

FATHER: No! You can't have the light on! Once upon a time there was a little girl who lived on the edge of a forest and her name was—

BRICE: Little Red Riding Hood.

FATHER: Yes. And one day her mother gave—

BRICE: Whose mother?

FATHER: Red Riding Hood's. She gave her a basket—

BRICE: She gave her mother?

FATHER: No! Her mother gave her a basket!

BRICE: Gave who?

FATHER: RED RIDING HOOD!

BRICE: Ohhhhh!

FATHER: Her mother gave her a basket—

BRICE: To take to her granny!

FATHER: Yes! She told her to take it to her grandmother—

BRICE: Because she was sick.

FATHER: If you know it so well why do you make me tell it to you?

BRICE: I like it.

FATHER: Well, don't interrupt and let me get thru! Before she left her mother told her not to talk to anybody in the woods, and—

BRICE: What woods?

FATHER: Where they lived!

BRICE: Who lived?

BOTH: (YELL) RED RIDING HOOD!

FATHER: Snooks, are you just trying to torment me? You know I'm dying for sleep.

BRICE: I won't do it again, daddy.

FATHER: All right. So Red Riding Hood took the basket of food and set off—

BRICE: For her granny's!

FATHER: Yes. On the way she met a terrible frightening ugly, shaggy looking beast—

BRICE: Uncle Louie!

FATHER: Ye—NO! It was a wolf!

BRICE: Who?

FATHER: Uncle Louie—I mean what she met! Don't interrupt me again. Red Riding Hood forgot what her mother told her about not wasting time or talking to anybody and when the wolf came along she was picking flowers. So, the wolf came over to her—

BRICE: (SNORES LIGHTLY)

FATHER: (QUIETLY PETERING OUT) and—started to get very friendly—

           (ALMOST A WHISPER) He said—

BRICE:	(SNORES)
FATHER:	She's asleep! Thank heaven - now I can rest .. (SETTLES)
BRICE:	(VERY BRIGHT) What did he say, daddy?
FATHER:	Huh? Who?
BRICE:	The wolf?
FATHER:	I thought you were sleeping! I can't tell you any more of the story.
BRICE:	Why?
FATHER:	Because the part about the wolf will scare you and you'll have unpleasant dreams.
BRICE:	Well, put the light on.
FATHER:	I will not—and you go to sleep this instant!
BRICE:	Waaahhh!
FATHER:	You can yell all you want. I won't put the light on!
BRICE:	Then finish the story.
FATHER:	All right - but if you get scared, don't blame me! The wolf crept up behind little Red Riding Hood—(GETS VERY EERIE) - with his long fang-like teeth protruding - his claws reaching out - his horrible eyes bulging—
BRICE:	(LAUGHS) Waaah!
FATHER:	You see! You're afraid!
BRICE:	No I ain't - I like it!
FATHER:	(TO HIMSELF) Oh, you do, eh? Well, I'll fix you…(TURNS ON THE HORROR VOICE)…The vicious wolf crept closer—and closer—to the poor child—his hair standing on end—a wild maniacal look on his demon face, bloodshot eyes—closer—closer—THUMP…THUMP…THUMP…He's reaching out his sharp claws to—(HIS VOICE SHAKES)—Snooks.
BRICE:	Huh?
FATHER:	Er—maybe you better put the light on.
BRICE:	Are you scared, daddy?
FATHER:	No, I'm not scared! I'm afraid you are, that's all.
BRICE:	I like it!
FATHER:	Well, I don't like it! And I'm going to sleep and so are you.

BRICE:	(COYLY) Oh, no I ain't!
FATHER:	(COYLY) Oh, yes you are!
BRICE:	(COYLY) Oh, no I ain't!
FATHER:	(MAD) Oh, maybe you'd like me to go sleep in the dog kennel!
BRICE:	Uh-huh!
FATHER:	(AGHAST) SNOOKS! How could you say a thing like that?
BRICE:	I didn't say it—you said it!
FATHER:	Why should I sleep in the dog kennel?
BRICE:	So the dog can sleep with me! (LAUGHS)
FATHER:	Why, you little—(SLAP)
BRICE:	WAAAAHHHHHH!

(MUSIC...APPLAUSE)

FIRST HALF OF SHOW

HULL:	Bob, it just occurred to me...I've been a frequent accomplice of yours in these *Good News* satires we've been perpetrating on the fair sex...and I'm beginning to wonder how well I stand with the ladies in our audience.
YOUNG:	Like "If men went shopping as women do," eh? Well, Warren, I'll bet you can improve your standing right now with a word or two of good advice...
HULL:	Ladies, suppose you were shopping for a dress and you saw one you liked, but its color was faded. Would you buy that dress? I'm pretty sure you'd say...
WOMAN'S VOICE:	(IN FAST) What a silly question. Of course I wouldn't buy it. No woman would *think* of buying a dress whose *color* has *faded*. She wouldn't be getting her money's worth.
HULL:	It does sound silly, all right. But, then, how about *coffee* whose *flavor* has faded. The next time you're at your grocer's and you notice that grand fragrance of coffee in the air, please remember ... it's the flavor and body of coffee *fading*, being *wasted*—flavor you'll never get in your cup. It's air, you know, that steals away coffee flavor. And all coffee, whether ground or in the whole bean, starts to lose flavor the

moment it's roasted, if exposed to the air. In fact, ground coffee packed in ordinary containers, where the air can get at it, loses as much as forty-five per cent...nearly half of its flavor in only nine days.

But not Maxwell House Coffee. Right there you have the reason why we take Maxwell House, still warm and fragrant from the roasting ovens, and pack it in the familiar, blue super-vacuum can. No *air* can get in—so no *flavor* can get out. Maxwell House comes right into your kitchen with all its wonderful flavor and fragrance sealed *in*—none wasted.

Not just days fresh, but...*roaster* fresh.

So treat yourself to a pound tomorrow, won't you? Today, with the marvelously enriched blend and new process of roasting, this *new* Maxwell House Coffee is more delicious, more downright satisfying than ever.

And, at today's prices, you'll discover that now is the time to...make friends with Maxwell House.

(MUSIC BRIDGE)

YOUNG: Now, a charming lady who has visited our Good News program before—Zarova, singing in Russian a song from the new Norma Shearer-Clark Gable picture, *Idiot's Delight*—entitled "How Strange."

"HOW STRANGE" – ZAROVA CHORUS AND ORCH.

APPLAUSE

MORGAN - YOUNG - DOUGLAS

YOUNG: That was marvelous! Miss Zarova—you must come back soon!

ZAROVA: Thank you!

YOUNG: We now return to the gloomier side of our Good News program—Part Two of the Douglas Diatribe. Professor Douglas!

(CHORD FROM ORCHESTRA)

DOUGLAS: I'm misunderstood.

YOUNG: Not at all, Doctor! You've diagnosed the complaint—now what about the prescription?

DOUGLAS: I have a very simple remedy—I'll show you how it works. Take any famous romantic meeting. I don't know exactly how or where Romeo first saw Juliet—but for pictures I would do it like this.

YOUNG:	Roll 'em.
DOUGLAS:	We're in the Capulet's garden. The moon is shining. At the edge of a shimmering pool which reflects her youthful charms—stands Juliet. Her soft, lovely hair is hanging down about her ivory shoulders. Can you see her?
YOUNG:	Yes.
DOUGLAS:	There she is—beautiful, young, unashamed.
MORGAN:	(COMING IN) Where is she? Let's have a look at her!
	(GIGGLES)
DOUGLAS:	Oh, Frank, you've spoiled the whole picture!
MORGAN:	Oh—pictures? Well, let's see 'em!
YOUNG:	Nobody's got any pictures! Haven't you been listening to what's going on?
MORGAN:	No, I've been down town, arguing with the people about my income tax. Had a terrible time.
DOUGLAS:	Frank—isn't it a little early to be worrying about your income tax?
MORGAN:	Er—tax—oh—this is my tax for 1929. Took me two hours to convince them that I was exempt that year.
YOUNG:	You didn't have to pay any tax in 1929, huh?
MORGAN:	Not a penny. I quote from the Federal Tax Statute of 1920 as amended, article six, section fourteen, paragraph A—
DOUGLAS:	Fifth floor, ladies corsets.
YOUNG:	Watch your step, please.
MORGAN:	Basement, all out! The article reads: "No employee of the United States government shall be subject to the Federal income tax, whereas hereinbefore—
YOUNG:	Frank! You were an employee of the Federal government in 1929?
MORGAN:	In a confidential capacity. Ah, those dangerous days!
YOUNG:	Confidential, huh? Were you in the secret service, Frank?
MORGAN:	No, my boy. Frank Morgan was the original G-Man. Single-handed, I founded the Federal Bureau of Investigation, organized a peerless squad of super sleuths, and built the department into the magnificent crime-catching organization we know today.
YOUNG:	What about Hoover?

MORGAN:	He was a fine president. My first assignment as a G-Man came from the state department—a highly secret mission. A government agent took me to New York and put me aboard the Aquitania. From then on I dropped my name and became a number. Operator 52—but the mission was so secret, I changed my number every day. I was 39 the second day, then 74, 48, 63, 67—
YOUNG and DOUGLAS:	(TOGETHER) Bingo!
MORGAN:	There will be two prizes, ladies and gentlemen, as customary in case of a tie. Well sir, I reached London, put up at a fashionable hotel, and for two years I remained there, disguised as an eccentric millionaire.
YOUNG:	I suppose you gave up wine, women and song?
MORGAN:	Er—no, I was just eccentric, not insane. But while to the superficial eye I was living the life of an irresponsible playboy, I was constantly aware of my dangerous secret mission. However, after two years I returned to the United States with the case still unsolved.
YOUNG:	What WAS the secret mission?
MORGAN:	Well, it was such a secret they didn't even tell _me_! I often wonder what it was.
DOUGLAS:	That must have finished you as a G-Man, Frank.
MORGAN:	On the contrary, my boy. I was promoted, because during the whole two years no one ever suspected I was a detective.
YOUNG:	Not even the government.
MORGAN:	(LOOKS AT HIM) Well, I can see you boys don't want to hear the story of my greatest triumph as a G-Man. (A SAD OLD MAN) All right—I'll go along. Not many places where I'm wanted, any more. (DEEP SIGH) Seems everybody's turning against me, these days. Well—
DOUGLAS:	(TOUCHED) Aw, wait a minute, Frank.
YOUNG:	Frank, I was only kidding!
DOUGLAS:	We want to hear the story!
YOUNG:	Sure we want to hear it!
MORGAN:	(VERY BRIGHT AGAIN) You really want to hear it?
DOUGLAS and YOUNG:	Sure. Yes!

MORGAN: Well gentlemen, I painted my greatest masterpiece while I was living—

YOUNG: Frank, you were telling us about your days as a G-Man…when you lived in Washington…and you were just going into the story of your greatest criminal case!

MORGAN: (MUMBLES) G-Man—Washington—case—whiskey—er—criminal—er—yes! In 1931 there was reported to the U.S. government a tremendous leak in the world diamond market. The same leak was discovered simultaneously in France, England and practically every country in Europe and Asia.

DOUGLAS: The leak of nations.

MORGAN: Precisely. (WITHERS HIM) Why don't you two boys team up and do a vaudeville act?

YOUNG: Go on with the diamonds, Frank.

MORGAN: Diamonds. Yes. I was assigned to the case, of course, and I sailed at once for Port Said.

YOUNG: The crooks were there.

MORGAN: No, they were in Paris, but I wanted to throw them off the track. Besides, I'd always wanted to see the town, and I look good in a pith helmet and shorts. While I was there, I thought I'd check over the pyramids and some of the sights of Egypt.

YOUNG: Sphinx?

MORGAN: Yes. I liked it pretty well. The only untoward incident was that I lost my favorite pith helmet - a gift from the Pasha of Sasha. I couldn't imagine where I'd left it. But you can understand that by the time I arrived in Paris, six months later, the crooks were pretty well off their guard.

YOUNG: You loaf for three months to throw them off their guard.

MORGAN: Who was loafing? During every moment of my spare time I was thinking—reasoning it out from A to Zee. When I reached Paris, I had the answer.

YOUNG: You knew the crook?

MORGAN: No, I remembered where I'd left my pith helmet. It was under my bed in the Shephards Hotel.

DOUGLAS: What about the diamond thieves, G-Man?

MORGAN: I soon pinned the crime on one darling, darling fellow—a famous international variety artist—a juggler, known as Jambon.

YOUNG: All right—did you hang it on him?

MORGAN: Patience, my boy! I called on Jambon in his dressing room at the Casino, and gave him an audition.

YOUNG: You juggled?

MORGAN: Like an angel! For fifteen minutes my Indian clubs flashed through the air in a maze of geometric patterns. Never a false move, never a slip—only perfection. Gentlemen, Jambon was a crook—but he was also an artist, and I swear to you that when I stopped, his eyes were filled with admiration. He paused for a moment, and said, "There is one thing more. Can you do the trick of the quatre trefles?"

YOUNG: What's that?

MORGAN: Four clubs.

YOUNG: Five hearts.

DOUGLAS: Six spades.

MORGAN: I pass. I performed the difficult trick without an instant's hesitation—and that night, a new team made its bow, at the Casino.—We were a sensation—but when we reached the climax of our act—a routine where we exchanged a hundred and fifty flying clubs at lightning speed—something happened.

YOUNG: You dropped a club!

MORGAN: Never! But when the fifty-fourth club struck my hand, I realized with my delicate touch that it must weigh at least ten milligrams more than any of the others.

YOUNG: How could you tell?

MORGAN: I used to be a weight guesser at Ocean Park. The minute I touched the club, I knew I'd solve the crime.

YOUNG: You got him! Go on, Frank.

MORGAN: We finished in a tumult of applause - I grabbed the fifty-fourth club, rushed to the dressing room, and hid behind the door.

YOUNG: He's gonna nail him!

MORGAN: Yes, as Libajola entered the room, I crashed the club down on his head, breaking the club in half and at the same time knocking him unconscious. Gentlemen—what do you think was in the Indian club?

BOTH: The diamonds!

MORGAN:	No—an Indian! He was a midget. Well, so long fellows. I've got to—
YOUNG:	Frank! An Indian midget!? What was he doing there?
MORGAN:	He had a fight with his squaw, and had to stay in his club. Well, so long boys—I'll see you later!

(APPLAUSE)

MUSIC UP

STATION BREAK

YOUNG:	And now it's time for our familiar Thursday evening custom…a moment of relaxation over a steaming, freshly made cup of…
DOUGLAS:	Here I am, Robert. And I've brought a very charming guest with me. Her name is Bruce.
YOUNG:	Why, Virginia. You and Melvyn are just in time for a cup of this coffee that's good to the last drop. It's an institution with us, you know…
BRUCE:	And an institution with me, too, Bob.
YOUNG:	Glad to hear it, Miss Bruce…Now Warren, let's pour out the Maxwell House. Here you are, Virginia…and Melvyn…and friends all over the country, pull up your chairs and join us in this friendly custom. Will you have cream…sugar? And Meredith, will you pour out the music?

(MUSIC UP AND FADE)

HULL:	We now pause briefly for station identification.

(MUSIC UP AND FADE)

AFTER BREAK

YOUNG:	This is Bob Young again, and we continue our Good News Maxwell House program with Melvyn Douglas and Virginia Bruce. Meredith Willson starts our second act with a tune from the new Jack Benny picture *Artists and Models*. You all know it—"What Have You Got That Gets Me."

"WHAT HAVE YOU GOT THAT GETS ME" – ORCHESTRA

APPLAUSE

YOUNG:	Meredith, you've started our second act very melodically—now stick around for the dramatic work.
MEREDITH:	Okay, Bob.

YOUNG: Our MGM Theater of the Air presentation tonight, as I told you before, is a triumphant return engagement of Melvyn Douglas and Virginia Bruce in a romantic playlet by the same young man who was responsible for their vehicle here two weeks ago. His name is Robert Riley Crutcher, and his play tonight is called "The Bohemian." Miss Bruce plays the part of Diane Sheridan, a rich young lady…Mr. Douglas plays the part of Alan Merrick, a poor young artist. Miss Sheridan is riding in a chauffeur-driven limousine as our play begins. They're just approaching Washington square, in New York City.

SKETCH

YOUNG: (OVER APPLAUSE) Thank you for a beautiful performance, Miss Bruce—and Mr. Douglas! They'll be back with us in a few moments, ladies and gentlemen—but now we hear again from the raven-haired song-bird of Beverly Hills—Tony Martin. This time Tony sings "This Night Will Be My Souvenir" from the M-G-M picture *Honolulu*.

SOUVENIR – MARTIN AND ORCHESTRA

APPLAUSE

SECOND HALF OF SHOW

YOUNG: Tony, that was grand. I always knew you could sing "good," as the boys say, but tonight…well, you really hit 'em…you were better than I've ever heard you.

MARTIN: Thanks very much, Robert. Matter of fact, I was about to make the same kind of remark to Warren Hull. I meant to tell you, Warren, that Alice and I have been really enjoying this new Maxwell House Coffee. We've always thought it was pretty swell before…but honestly, this new coffee is tops.

HULL: We think so, too, Tony. Not just because more and more people are saying nice things like that about Maxwell House. But because of two remarkable new improvements we've been able to make—both of them so important that Maxwell House today is truly a *new* coffee.

First of all, after months of effort and experiment, we've succeeded in enriching the famous blend of selected coffees that first made Maxwell House world-famous. The *new* Maxwell House today has an extra measure of goodness…an extra satisfying flavor you'll discover in your very first steaming, fragrant cup.

Then, we've also developed a new way of roasting Maxwell House, called "Radiant Roast"—an amazing process which roasts each coffee bean evenly all the way *through*—and so brings out the true, natural flavor of this superb new blend. This way there's no chance of weak coffee due to under-roasting, or bitter coffee due to parching. Your new Maxwell House is always full-bodied, always smooth and mellow.

Friends, into every pound of Maxwell House Coffee goes more than fifty years experience in the art of coffee-blending and roasting...And our never-ending efforts to bring you the utmost in true coffee enjoyment.

Today we believe the *new* Maxwell House is just about the finest coffee you've ever tasted. And we're pretty sure you'll agree...because more people are buying Maxwell House today than ever before in its history.

So, if *you* haven't tried it lately, why not order a pound? We think you'll say this *new* Maxwell House is more than ever...good to the last drop.

(MUSIC BRIDGE)

DOUGLAS – BRUCE – YOUNG – WILLSON

YOUNG: Meredith Willson's concert hall tonight has a guest of honor...Miss Virginia Bruce. Virginia, before we get down to the weighty musical matters, may I say I enjoyed your performance with Melvyn?

BRUCE: Thank you. I thought Melvyn was wonderful. Especially considering he doesn't like things to be romantic.

DOUG: Who doesn't? I love it! I never run into it, that's all.

YOUNG: Neither do I—but I believe in it. I'll bet Virginia has had some romantic rescues, or something.

DOUGLAS: Oh sure. Virginia, were you ever rescued from the edge of a cliff—or pulled out from a sawmill in the nick of time by a handsome hero? Or saved in a steamship disaster?

BRUCE: I was once rescued from drowning. It was one summer on the Riviera, and I owe my life to Michel Francois Charbonnier, the Seoond.

YOUNG: He rescued you, huh?

BRUCE: Without a moment's hesitation. I wasn't a very strong swimmer at the time, and I had got out beyond my depth. I called for help, and I saw Michel plunge into the surf. He swam toward me steadily, and reached my side just as I was losing consciousness. How he managed to get me ashore I'll never know.

YOUNG:	Did you fall in love with him?
BRUCE:	Instantly. We went to Paris, and he never left my side. When it was time to go home, I couldn't bear the thought of leaving him—so he came with me—and he's living with us now.
DOUGLAS:	Virginia! Doesn't your husband object?
BRUCE:	Melvyn, who could object to a French Poodle?
YOUNG:	Well, that winds up the romance for today. Now Virginia—Meredith Willson has a musical question for you.
BRUCE:	All right.
MERE:	Miss Bruce—if all the music in the world had been destroyed and you could choose just one composition to hear again and preserve—what would you choose?
BRUCE:	Could you give me just a hint, Meredith?
MERE:	Well— seven hundred students at Lansdowne High School, in Lansdowne, Pennsylvania, have voted for Schubert's Marche Militaire—and we've been rehearsing it.
BRUCE:	What an amazing coincidence! That's the one piece I'm dying to hear!
YOUNG:	I guess that rounds out everything nicely. Ladies and gentlemen, Meredith Willson plays Schubert's Marche Militaire.
	MARCHE MILITAIRE – ORCH.
	CLAP
YOUNG:	That's about all for tonight, ladies and gentlemen, but—
BARRYMORE:	Excuse me, Bob. Do you mind if I interrupt?
YOUNG:	Mr. Lionel Barrymore, it's a pleasure.
BARRYMORE:	As a member of your studio audience I'd like to congratulate you on your show tonight. Fine piece of entertainment all around.
YOUNG:	Thank you Lionel—on behalf of everybody. I suppose you know that people are still talking about the last time that YOU were on the program. They all want you back again.
BARRYMORE:	That's very gratifying, Bob.
YOUNG:	You remember I asked you last week if you could think of anything you wanted to do. Have you found anything yet?
BARRYMORE:	I have, but I don't think it's going to be practical.
YOUNG:	Why not?

BARRYMORE: In the first place it's a sketch about Lincoln—

YOUNG: Well you're the best Lincoln I ever saw!

BARRYMORE: Thank you—but that's not the main difficulty. This particular sketch needs a magnificent youthful actor to work with Lincoln—

YOUNG: (CLEAR THROAT) Well er—how about a semi-magnificent actor—like me?

BARRYMORE: (LAUGHS) You'd be fine, Bob—except you're not young enough.

DOUGLAS: Well—how about me?

BARRYMORE: I need someone even younger than you, Melvyn.

YOUNG: If Morgan volunteers, I'll hit him with a stick. How old must this youthful actor be, Lionel?

BARRYMORE: Well, around fifteen, sixteen years old.

ROONEY: Say! That part sounds like it's for Rooney, boys - step aside!

YOUNG: Mickey Rooney!

(APPLAUSE)

YOUNG: Lionel, Mickey would be great. How about it?

BARRYMORE: Yes, he would. Shall we get together, Mickey?

ROONEY: My time is your time, Pop.

YOUNG: That's how we plan our Good News program, ladies and gentlemen. Next week, Lionel Barrymore and Mickey Rooney in a sketch about Abraham Lincoln. Also—Fanny Brice and Hanley Stafford, Frank Morgan, Douglas McPhail, and Meredith Willson. Be on the lookout for Norma Shearer and Clark Gable in M-G-M's new sensational motion picture, "Idiot's Delight." See you next Thursday—and in the meantime, go to the movies and take the family with you. This is Bob Young saying Goodnight.

HULL: (CREDITS)

This is Warren Hull saying goodnight and good luck for the makers of Maxwell House—the coffee that's always good to the last drop—

THIS IS THE NATIONAL BROADCASTING COMPANY.

POST TOASTIES TIME
JUNE 18, 1942

1. SNOOKS AND DADDY OPENER

2. THEME....CAST INTRO

"LAST CALL FOR LOVE"

3. FRANK MORGAN SPOT

4. MIDDLE COMMERCIAL

5. "WALTZ IN A FLAT"

6. BABY SNOOKS SPOT

7. CLOSING COMMERCIAL

8. THEME...SIGN-OFF

9. HITCH-HIKE

BRICE:	Daddy!
FATHER:	Snooks, please let me read my magazine in peace for a few minutes.
BRICE:	I wanna ask you something.
FATHER:	Well, what is it?
BRICE:	How old am I?
FATHER:	Seven. You were seven years old on February 22.
BRICE:	Why?
FATHER:	Because that's when you were born. On George Washington's birthday.
BRICE:	Is George Washington seven years old?
FATHER:	No! If George Washington had lived he'd be two hundred and ten years old.
BRICE:	How old would I be if I lived?

FATHER:	Go away and let me read.
BRICE:	What are you reading, daddy?
FATHER:	A magazine!
BRICE:	Has it got pictures of pretty—
FATHER:	I don't care about the pictures! This is a magazine of current world events and it's called Time!
BRICE:	Why?
FATHER:	Because that's its name! Will you leave me alone?
BRICE:	Well, what's the name of the magazine?
FATHER:	Time! Time! Time!
BRICE:	Three times?
FATHER:	No—one Time!
BRICE:	Does it tick?
FATHER:	It doesn't tick! It's paper and it's not like the other kind of them!
BRICE:	Well, what kind of time is it?
WILCOX:	(HOLLERS) It's Post Toasties Time!
	(THEME...APPLAUSE)
HARLOW:	Yes, ladies and gentlemen, it's that familiar time once again, and your regular Thursday evening gloom dispellers are all here to dish out a little joy. Of course, Frank Morgan is still suffering from his attack of amnesia, but he's got company in the person of Groucho Marx who is also in the same sorry plight. Then there's Meredith Willson and his music, Hanley Stafford as Daddy, and Fanny Brice as the incomparable Baby Snooks. All these delightful people will be kept in line by our master of ceremonies—your host for the evening—John Conte!
	"LAST CALL FOR LOVE" – CONTE & ORCH
	(APPLAUSE)
CONTE:	Thank you, ladies and gentlemen, and good evening. Those of you who listened to this program last week are probably wondering why Harlow didn't announce Jimmy Durante's name along with the others.
MERE:	I knew it! I knew it!
CONTE:	You knew what, Meredith?

MERE: Jimmy Durante's not gonna be here tonight!

CONTE: That's an amazing piece of deduction. How did you arrive at the conclusion, Dithy?

MERE: I knew it the minute I listened to Harlow and heard Jimmy Durante's name not announced!

CONTE: How could you hear Jimmy Durante's name if it wasn't announced?

MERE: That's just it. I heard him not announce it as clear as a bell! It's like if you like radishes and you have 'em for dinner every Friday, and one Friday they're not on the table—the first thing you don't see is the radishes because you're not really looking for them.

CONTE: Did Harlow say anything about radishes?

MERE: No—that's why I missed 'em. Although I don't know why I'm worried because we don't have radishes except only on Friday nights and it's still Thursday, isn't it?

CONTE: I don't know what month it is!

MERE: Well, you're just a little confused, John.

CONTE: I'm confused!

MERE: Sure—you're upset on account of Harlow not announcing the radishes. What was the reason for it, John?

CONTE: We're out of salt.

MERE: Oh. Well, I can take 'em with or without. It's a funny thing—

CONTE: Meredith! How you got into radishes I'll never know—the only thing that matters is that I must tell the people why Jimmy Durante isn't going to be here tonight!

MERE: He isn't? Jeepers—why didn't you say something about it?

CONTE: I'm going to right now! Ladies and gentlemen, there's a lot of explaining to be done. To begin with, two weeks ago Frank Morgan got an attack of amnesia. The doctor who was present prescribed constant conversation with old friends to restore Frank's memory.

MERE: Yes—and it don't work. I've talked to every old friend I know and poor Frank sits there just as blank as ever. I don't know where these—

CONTE: He wanted Frank to talk to old friends—not you! That's why we had Groucho Marx here last week.

MERE: Sure—and what happened? The minute Groucho went into Frank's dressing room he got amnesia, too.

CONTE: That's the mysterious part of it. But right after that I phoned Jimmy Durante and asked him to be here tonight. He agreed to come and then he got an urgent call to be in New York. Well, he went and yesterday I received a telegram from him telling me he couldn't return on schedule.

MERE: What did he say?

CONTE: Well, he said it was impossible for him to return due to a concatenation of events growing from governmental demands on transportation facilities.

MERE: Jimmy Durante said that?

CONTE: Words to that effect.

MERE: Let me see the telegram.

CONTE: Here.

MERE: (READS) Dear John. Headed westward by plane but was grounded in Palm Springs. My nose landed in Banning but my heart and soul is with you. Love, Schnozzola!

CONTE: Maybe he'll be here next week. But in the meantime we have to do something about Frank.

MERE: And Groucho.

CONTE: Yes. I have a feeling the minute we cure Frank Groucho will snap out of it, too. What can we do?

MERE: Shall we try and talk to him? Remind him of familiar things?

CONTE: I've got it! His boat! He loved his boat more than anything in the world. We'll keep talking to him about his boat.

MERE: Sure! I bet she'll bring his memory back! I'll never forget how he adored her. Every time he took her out he polished her funnels with oily rags.

MORGAN: (COMING ON) Well, every man has his little quirks—besides, the girl was crazy about it. (LAUGHS)

CONTE: Frank! Frank Morgan!

(APPLAUSE)

MORGAN: What's the matter with you, Jockey? You act like you've never seen me before.

CONTE: I can't talk.

MORGAN: Well, I hope it's nothing temporary. And you, Meredith—

MERE: Frank. You—you know who we are.

MORGAN: Know who you are? I regret to say I'm forced to admit to a nodding acquaintance-ship with both of you, unsavory as it is, but why should I start denying it now?

CONTE: Frank. This is a shock—you do recognize us. After what you've just been thru. How did you come out of it?

MORGAN: Now, look here, Jockey! If you're trying to imply that I'm not in full possession of my faculties, I resent it! You've already given me a reputation for imbibing which is impossible to live down—especially when I live up to it. But why you should—

CONTE: Wait a minute, Frank. Do you know that you've had a case of amnesia!

FRANK: I had amnesia?

MERE: Sure, Frank. You didn't know anybody for two whole weeks!

MORGAN: (LAUGHS) Are you serious, Jockey?

CONTE: He's not Jockey—I'm Jockey !

MERE: Jeepers, don't go off again, Frank. Look at me—I'm Meredith. Meredith Willson—two ells. I lead the band.

MORGAN: Oh—lead the band—two ells. I wish I knew why you're both displaying this consternation.

CONTE: Listen, Frank. Two weeks ago you attempted to do a little mass hypnotism. Before you got to it you lost your memory and you've been sitting in that dressing room ever since.

MORGAN: Did you call a doctor?

MERE: There was a doctor here—don't you remember—Dr. Drake?

MORGAN: Oh, yes—Drake. Sort of a funny duck. I remember now. But I don't remember anything about the two weeks that you say have passed.

CONTE: Naturally you wouldn't. What brought you out of your amnesia?

MORGAN: It's all very hazy. But I do recall sitting in my dressing room a few minutes ago and there was a knock at the door.

MERE: Uh-huh.

MORGAN: I opened it and there was a charming young lady standing on the threshold. She was selling magazines.

CONTE:	Magazines?
MORGAN:	Yes. Working her way thru burlesque, I believe she said. At any rate, I purchased her entire stock of magazines. A half a dozen Colliers, three Redbooks, five Lifes, and before she went I took a couple of Looks.
CONTE:	Did you take any Libertys?
MORGAN:	Well, I tried to hold her hand but she—oh ! Libertys ! You mean the magazine!
CONTE:	Yes!
MORGAN:	No—she'd already sold out. Well, I think I'll go and read one of—
CONTE:	Wait ! You can't leave here until we solve the mystery of this amnesia, Frank.
MORGAN:	There's no mystery, my boy. (DRAMATICALLY) I'm going to reveal something to you that my grandfather first disclosed to me with bated breath. And I don't have to tell you what his breath was baited with.
MERE:	What is it, huh, Frank? Huh? What is it, huh? Huh?
MORGAN:	Patience, Meredith. I've long been expecting this sudden attack—and for many years I've been living in terror.
CONTE:	You've been living in terror?
MORGAN:	Terror Haute, Indiana. We moved from there while I was still in my swaddling clothes but not soon enough to escape the dread curse of the Morgans. Pharkleigh's Disease—better known as recurrent amnesia.
MERE:	Jeeps—I got the creeps. (SHUDDERS)
CONTE:	Is it hereditary, Frank?
MORGAN:	Only on the male side of the family. The women have other rare ailments but this is no time to discuss it. However, most doctors believe that recurrent amnesia is brought about by the seventh phase of the moon cycle while completing its orbit in the vernal equinox. Do you understand that, Jockey?
CONTE:	Perfectly.
MORGAN:	Er—then I'll try something else. Personally, I don't agree with the doctors' explanation, since I know the history of the first attack.
MERE:	Tell us about the first attank, Frank.

MORGAN: Attankfrack?

MERE: I mean affracktank—you know what I mean.

MORGAN: I think so. It all began with an excavating party in Egypt long before I was born. The expedition was headed by my grandfather, Pyramid Morgan, and they were searching for the sarcophagus that contained the remains of King Rameses the First.

CONTE: What did he want with it?

MORGAN: Well, King Rameses was the heaviest of all Egyptian kings—weighing six hundred pounds without his toga.

MERE: What did his toga weigh?

MORGAN: History records Rameses as possessing a toga that weighed ninety pounds—but that's a pretty broad statement. However, we do know he was the daddy of all mummies.

CONTE: I know—but what did you grandfather want his remains for?

MORGAN: It was rumored that buried in the sarcophagus was the secret formula for mummifying women. My gaffer had an extremely talkative wife—and he was looking for a way to make her dry up. (That sounds pretty flimsy to me, too.)

MERE: Not to me, boy! Did he ever find the remains?

MORGAN: He did. After many months of exploring the tombs he finally came to an Egyptian settlement known as a Toopehr.

CONTE: Toopehr—what's that?

MORGAN: Oasis and tents.

CONTE: You win—I got jacks and fifes.

MORGAN: That's the first pot I've won all—what are we talking about!

MERE: You cut that out, John! Go on, Frank.

MORGAN: Where was I?

CONTE: In the tombs.

MORGAN: Yes. I did thirty days there for a disorderly conduct rap and my lawyer—what am I saying?

CONTE: I'm sorry, Frank. Let's get back to Egypt. Where did your father find this sarcophagus of Rameses?

MORGAN: Right where he was buried. There he was shrouded in his wrappings, and covered from head to foot with precious gems, lying peacefully inside a famous Egyptian structure.

CONTE:	Sphinx?
MORGAN:	A little. What can you expect from a man who's been buried for three thousand years? Well, the search was ended and—
CONTE:	Wait a minute. What about the amnesia? How did that start?
MORGAN:	A curse had been placed upon the tomb—and it struck instantly. My gaffer immediately lost his memory and every Morgan thereafter has been subject to the same attack. That's the story, gentlemen.
MERE:	You mean you might get it again?
MORGAN:	It's very possible—but you need have no fear. When I found out I was afflicted with this terrible threat I scoured the world for an antidote. And I found it!
CONTE:	Well, thank heaven for that. If it ever hits you again what shall we do?
MORGAN:	It's simplicity itself—and the antidote cannot fail. If I should suffer another attack of amnesia, all you have to do is—is—(STOPS AND LOOKS BLANKLY AT THEM)
MERE:	What's the matter, Frank?
MORGAN:	Frank?
CONTE:	Morgan! What's the antidote—quick!
MORGAN:	Antidote? Who are you, young man? What am I doing here?
MERE:	(CRYING) He's got it again!
MORGAN:	I want to lie down.
CONTE:	Ohhhh—we're cooked! Take him away, Meredith.
MERE:	(CRYING) Hang on to my arm, Frank. Come on.
MORGAN:	Why do you keep calling me Frank, young man? Who is that other chap and how did I get here?
	(THEY AD LIB OFF THE STAGE)
CONTE:	Ladies and gentlemen, I'm offering a reward of three hundred million dollars for anybody who knows the antidote that Frank was about to tell us. Play something, fellows.
	(MUSIC...APPLAUSE)

MIDDLE COMMERCIAL

(ORCH: BULLARD'S "WINTER SONG" – CONTE SINGS)

CONTE:	Oh! A song by the fire. Pass the pipes! Pass the bowl! Oh! A song by the fire. With a skoal! With a…
WILCOX:	Hold everything! Hold everything! Look John! And you, Meredith! Are you, by any chance, an alumni of Dartmouth?
CONTE & MERE:	(IN CHORUS) Nope!
WILCOX:	Then what's the idea? What on earth made you think of Bullard's "Winter Song" on a hot day, like this?
MERE:	Breakfast, Harlow! Breakfast.
WILCOX:	Breakfast? What in the world has Bullard's "Winter Song" got to do with a hot-weather breakfast?
MERE:	Well, a crisp, crisp, crackling fire sounds like this…
	(SOUND: CRISP, CRACKLING FIRE…)
WILCOX:	Yes! But go on! I don't get the connection.
	(START COMMERCIAL TIME HERE…)
	(MUSIC)
MERE:	Well…doesn't that crisp, crackling sound remind you of a certain crisp cereal? Eh, Harlow, old kid? Eh, Harlow!
WILCOX:	(CUE LINE) Yes, since you've put it in that way…it does!
	(SLIGHT PAUSE)
	(LOCAL STATIONS CUE-IN INSTANTANEOUSLY WITH POST'S RAISIN BRAN MIDDLE COMMERCIAL HERE)
WILCOX:	The crispest corn flakes on the market…Post Toasties! A bowlful of these crisper, more delicious corn flakes…topped with juicy-ripe, sun-sweetened berries…certainly starts the morning right…winter or summer.
MERE:	That's tellin' 'em, Harlow! That's tellin' 'em!
WILCOX:	Yes! And, housewives from coast to coast will back me up, because seventy per cent of those who tested corn flakes proved…right in their own kitchens…that Post Toasties stay crisper in milk…right down to the last delicious spoonful! What's the reason, you ask?

MERE:	Just a second, Harlow…let us tell them…with music!
ORCH:	"I'M FOREVER BLOWING BUBBLES"…BLAST THE BUBBLES IN BRASS…FOUR BARS, FOUR SECONDS
WILCOX:	That's it…bubbles…dozens of tiny bubbles of golden goodness on each and every flavorsome flake. Those bubbles mean that Post Toasties are bubbling over with crispness, and that they keep their tempting crispness longer in milk than ordinary corn flakes…they're appetized for crispness!
MERE:	It sure does make a difference, folks!
WILCOX:	So friends…why not brighten up your breakfast…why not give the slip to the hot-weather slump in your appetite…by making a morning habit of the crispiest corn flakes you ever tasted? I mean…Post Toasties!
	(PLAYOFF)
CONTE:	That was swell, Meredith. And now, ladies and—
STAFF:	Good evening, John.
CONTE:	Hello, daddy. How are the twins?
STAFF:	Wonderful. I'd like you to come to the christening next week.
CONTE:	Wouldn't miss it for the world. What have you decided to name them?
STAFF:	Well—I'd rather not say anything now. I want it to be a surprise.
CONTE:	Oh. It undoubtedly will be. How's Snooks behaving towards the babies?
STAFF:	Still a trifle distant—buy it's only natural. Even Robespierre is beginning to show resentment. I caught the little rascal squirting fly-spray at them. (LAUGHS)
CONTE:	(LAUGHS) Oh, what a delightful sense of humor. Do you have a nurse to take care of the twins?
STAFF:	No, I let her go last Monday. And believe me, I've got my hands full making their formulas and bathing them and everything.
CONTE:	Bathing them? You mean you actually give those little things a bath?
STAFF:	Certainly. Last night I decided to give them their first bath. I got the tub ready and sent Snooks to the drug store for some baby powder. On the way home she picked up Red and brought him back. I was busy in the bathroom and didn't hear them come in—(FADES)—but they sneaked into the nursery and—

(SNOOKS PLAY-ON)

BRICE: Now, don't make no noise, Red.

BOY: Okay. Where are they?

BRICE: Right there in those two cribs.

BOY: What are they—boys or girls?

BRICE: Half and half. That one's a boy—and that one's a girl.

BOY: How do you know?

BRICE: Daddy said you can tell by the blankets.

BOY: Blankets?

BRICE: Yeah. The boy has the blue blanket and the girl has the pink one.

BOY: Well, how do you tell if they ain't wearing no blankets?

BRICE: I dunno. Shall we fool daddy?

BOY: How?

BRICE: We'll change the blankets then he won't know which is which.

BOY: I got a better idea. Let's switch the kids.

BRICE: Okay—get a switch.

BOY: No, I don't mean that. They're too little to hit.

BRICE: You think so.

BOY: Sure. Besides, we ain't worn Robespierre out yet.

BRICE: Robespierre's getting awful big, Red.

BOY: Well, the two of us can handle him. Hey, what's these kids' names?

BRICE: I don't know the boy's name but I think the girl is called Helen Maria.

BOY: Helen Maria.

BRICE: That's what daddy says every time she wakes him up.

BOY: Don't sound like much of a name to me.

BRICE: Me neither. I call 'em both stinky.

BOY: Do they bawl much?

BRICE: Only when they're hungry. And they eat forty times a day.

BOY: I guess it'll cost me a pretty penny—but a deal's a deal. Which one do you wanna trade?

BRICE:	Take the boy. He's uglier.
BOY:	Go on—he ain't no uglier than the girl. She looks like you.
BRICE:	Well, take the girl then.
BOY:	No—I think I'll take the boy.
BRICE:	Awight. When do I get the kittens?
BOY:	You can come and get 'em now if you like. You think that crib'll hold nine kittens?
BRICE:	Is there only nine? You said there was ten.
BOY:	Well, I counted wrong.
BRICE:	Then I ain't gonna trade. Besides, daddy might get mad.
BOY:	What's he gonna got mad for? He's got plenty of kids but he ain't got no cats, has he?
BRICE:	No.
BOY:	Well?
BRICE:	Maybe we can teach one of the twins to catch mice.
BOY:	Okay, if you don't wanna trade. I better get out of here before your old man starts–
	(DOOR OPENS)
FATHER:	Snooks! When did you get — Red! What are you doing in the nursery?
BOY:	Hello, Mr. Higgins. Snooks just brought me in to look at the new babies. They're beautiful, Mr. Higgins.
FATHER:	(PLEASED) Do you really think so?
BOY:	Yeah. If they had a mustache they'd look just like you.
BRICE:	The girl's got a mustache.
FATHER:	Nonsense. That's just from her milk. As soon as I bathe her that'll disappear.
BRICE:	Will she disappear too?
FATHER:	I hope not. Er—where's the powder?
BRICE:	Powder?
FATHER:	I sent you to the drugstore for some powder for the babies.
BRICE:	Oh. They didn't have no gunpowder so I—

FATHER:	I didn't send you for gunpowder!
BRICE:	Flea powder?
FATHER:	No! I sent you for talcum powder. What happened?
BRICE:	Tell him Red.
FATHER:	What does he know about it?
BOY:	I went with her, Mr. Higgins. And when we got to the drugstore there was an awful big line there. And we had to stand on the end of the line.
BRICE:	Yeah.
FATHER:	If it was so crowded why didn't you go to another store?
BRICE:	'Cause I forgot what you wanted.
FATHER:	You forgot? Then why didn't you come home and find out?
BOY:	We didn't wanna lose our turn, Mr. Higgins.
FATHER:	That's ridiculous. What sense is there is standing in line and waiting for your turn if you didn't know what I wanted?
BRICE:	Well, we knew what *we* wanted. Have a jelly bean, daddy?
FATHER:	No! And I'll punish you for that as soon as I'm through bathing the twins. You go home, Red.
BOY:	Yes sir. Goodnight, Snooks.
BRICE:	Goodnight, Red. (WHISPERS) If you find the other kitten come back.
BOY:	(WHISPERS) Okay.
	(DOOR CLOSES)
FATHER:	Move out of my way, Snooks—I've got work to do.
BRICE:	Have you got the bathtub full?
FATHER:	Yes. But I don't know what I'm going to use for powder.
BRICE:	What do they need powder for, daddy?
FATHER:	To make their bodies smooth.
BRICE:	Why don't you rub 'em with sandpaper?
FATHER:	Sandpaper! Maybe you'd like to see me trim their nails with a hatchet!
BRICE:	Yeah—Let's do it, daddy. I'll hold 'em still and you—

FATHER:	Oh, stop it! I better got busy before the water gets too cool.
BRICE:	Are you gonna put both in together?
FATHER:	No. I think I'll take the boy first.
BRICE:	What are you gonna do with him?
FATHER:	Put him in the water, of course.
BRICE:	Can I drown the girl?
FATHER:	Drown her! You don't think I'm going to drown this baby, do you? Do you?
BRICE:	Uh-huh.
FATHER:	You're out of your mind. Go fetch me a towel—quick.
BRICE:	Where's the towels, daddy?
FATHER:	In the linen closet. Bring it to me in the bathroom.
BRICE:	Do you want a boy towel or a girl towel?
FATHER:	There's no such thing!
BRICE:	Well, one is pink and one is blue.
FATHER:	Okay—bring one of each. Hurry...Now—easy little feller...Hmm—he doesn't even wake up. I'll have you bathed and back in bed without you even knowing it. Let's get these things off.
BRICE:	Here's the towels, daddy.
FATHER:	Thank you. Put them down on the hamper and leave the bathroom.
BRICE:	Why?
FATHER:	Because ladies don't watch gentlemen while they're bathing.
BRICE:	Why?
FATHER:	Oh, all right. Just don't get in my way.
BRICE:	Can I get in the water with him?
FATHER:	Don't be silly. There isn't room for the two of you.
BRICE:	I'll sit on top of him.
FATHER:	No!
BRICE:	Then just let me gargle my feet in the tub.
FATHER:	Please step aside, Snooks—I'm going to put him in...(LIGHT SPLASH)...There we are!

BRICE: He don't even holler, daddy.

FATHER: That's because I got the temperature of the water just right. If the water's too hot the baby turns red.

BRICE: Do you cook 'em like lobsters?

FATHER: You don't cook them at all. The excessive heat of the water will cause the skin to turn a deeper red than it is. If the water's too cold—the baby will turn blue.

BRICE: He's turning white, daddy.

FATHER: Of course. You know what that means, don't you?

BRICE: Yeah—he needed the bath.

FATHER: No—it means the water's just right. (SPLASH)...That's enough, little man...Hand me a towel, Snooks.

BRICE: What for?

FATHER: I want to dry him.

BRICE: Why don't you hang him on the clothesline?

FATHER: Give me a towel! Hurry—the child is slippery.

BRICE: Here, daddy.

FATHER: Thanks...Have to dry them very gently. You'd better watch this, Snooks—some day you may have to do it.

BRICE: When?

FATHER: Oh, when you're a wife and a mother.

BRICE: Are you a wife and a mother, daddy?

FATHER: No. Mummy is.

BRICE: Is she your mother?

FATHER: She's my wife!

BRICE: Why?

FATHER: Because I married her.

BRICE: Why?

FATHER: I'll tell you why! (BELLIGERENT) Because I loved her and I still love her. Now, what are you gonna do about it?

BRICE: Don't worry—I won't tell her, daddy.

FATHER: She knows it. Now, you go on to bed while I bathe the other one.

BRICE:	Can't I watch?
FATHER:	You've already watched me bathe the boy. It'll be just the same with the girl.
BRICE:	Will it?
FATHER:	Yes.
BRICE:	Well, just let me watch while you undress her.
FATHER:	What for?
BRICE:	'Cause I never seen a girl barefoot all over.
FATHER:	You'll see her some other time. I've got to get this baby under the covers. Goodnight, Snooks.
BRICE:	Goodnight, daddy.
	(DOOR OPENS AND CLOSES)
BOY:	(WHISPERS) Hey, Snooks—I got 'em! Lookit!
	(KITTENS MIEOW)
BRICE:	How'd you get back in, Red?
BOY:	I left the front door open. You want the kittens?
BRICE:	Have you got ten of them?
BOY:	Yeah—this black one is a little dead but that don't matter.
BRICE:	Let's give 'em a bath.
BOY:	No—I gotta get out before your old man ruins the deal. Where's the kid?
BRICE:	He's in his crib. Daddy just washed him.
BOY:	Do I get his rubber pants, too?
BRICE:	Uh-huh. Don't let daddy hear us going into the nursery.
BOY:	Okay...(DOOR OPENS)...I wonder why they wear rubber pants.
BRICE:	I think it's in case you take 'em out in the rain.
	(KITTENS MIEOW)
BOY:	Shh—shh—little kitties...(THEY MIEOW LOUDER)
BRICE:	Shut up, you darn old cats! Here's the kid. Give me the cats.
BOY:	Okay. Help me lift—
FATHER:	(CALLS) Snooks—are you in the nursery?

BOY:	I'm going. I'll come back for the kid some other time…So long!
FATHER:	Snooks! Is that you in the nursery?
	(KITTENS MIEOW)
BRICE:	There ain't nobody here except us kittens, daddy.
FATHER:	Kittens? What on earth—Snooks! Where did the kittens come from?
BRICE:	I think the cat had them.
FATHER:	How do they come to be in here?
BRICE:	Well—I—er—Red just brought 'em over. We was gonna make a deal.
FATHER:	A deal? Snooks! You weren't going to trade the baby for those kittens! You weren't!
BRICE:	Wasn't I?
FATHER:	Oh, no! How could you think of such a dreadful thing?
BRICE:	I didn't think of it—Red thought of it.
FATHER:	I don't understand it. What does he want with the baby?
BRICE:	Well, you said he was a bouncing baby, didn't you?
FATHER:	What of it?
BRICE:	Red was gonna take him to the gas station and get a cent a pound for him.
FATHER:	Ohhh! And you were willing to be an accessory to this crime?
BRICE:	I knew he'd bring him back, daddy.
FATHER:	How did you know?
BRICE:	'Cause I tried it with the girl this morning.
FATHER:	You little—(SOCK)
BRICE:	WAAAAAAAHHHHH!
FATHER:	Go to bed!
	CLOSING COMMERCIAL
BRICE:	Daddy!
FATHER:	Yes! What is it?
BRICE:	Mummy had an epicure today!
FATHER:	A what?

BRICE:	An epicure! Her feet hurt, so she went to the foot doctor and had an epicure.
FATHER:	You don't mean epicure, my child! You mean pedicure.
BRICE:	Do I?
FATHER:	Yes! Epicure is a name bestowed on a person who is given to dainty indulgence in the pleasures of the table. It's from the Greek.
BRICE:	Is that why there are so many Greek restaurants?
FATHER:	Of course not! Epicurus was a Greek philosopher who was fond of good food.
BRICE:	Daddy! Let's be exp-curious?
FATHER:	Epi-curious?
	(START COMMERCIAL TIME HERE…)
BRICE:	Yeah! Let's sneak out to the pantry and be curious about how much of that crisp cereal it takes to cure our appetites.
FATHER:	(CUE LINE) What are we waiting for, Snooks? C'mon … let's go!
	(SLIGHT PAUSE)
	(LOCAL STATIONS CUT-IN INSTANTANEOUSLY WITH POST'S RAISIN BRAN CLOSING HERE…)
WILCOX:	Hey! Wait for me—Daddy! Post Toasties…bubbling over with crispness…packed with the mellow flavor of sun-ripened, toasted corn…mighty good eating, I'll say!
BRICE:	You know what Mother Goose says…
WILCOX:	And, for an extra-special treat, try crisper Post Toasties with your favorite fresh berries and cream. There's a marvelous dish for a hot-weather lunch—or a bed-time snack. No matter when you eat Post Toasties, they're light yet nourishing…easy to digest…completely satisfying!
BRICE:	Mother Goose says…
WILCOX:	Why not find out how downright delicious really crisp corn flakes taste? Tomorrow, ask your grocer for Post Toasties…the crisper corn flakes! And now…what does Mother Goose say, Snooks?
BRICE:	Rock-a-bye, baby, on the tree top. When the wind blows the cradle will rock. When he gets hungry baby will scream, And mummy will give him Post Toasties and cream.

(LAUGHS) I like 'em.

(EASTERN BROADCAST ONLY)

HITCH-HIKE

BINGMAN: Beat the heat with a salad treat! Something new in *fruit* salads. Fresh plums stuffed with cream cheese and ginger...arranged on lettuce with orange slices. Serve with HELLMANN'S or BEST FOODS REAL MAYONNAISE mixed with a little pineapple juice! Boy, oh boy, *real* mayonnaise has a way with salads! Because it's not ordinary salad dressing...but all mayonnaise...made like the home kind, with no starchy filler! Really fresh...Really delicious! Better try HELLMANN'S or BEST FOODS REAL MAYONNAISE!

This program came to you from Hollywood.

THIS IS THE NATIONAL BROADCASTING COMPANY

MAXWELL HOUSE PRESENTS
"GOOD NEWS OF 1939"
JANUARY 5, 1939
#54

CAST

1. Warren Hull
2. Robert Young
3. Virginia Bruce
4. Melvyn Douglas
5. Douglas MacPhail
6. Frank Morgan
7. Fanny Brice
8. Hanley Stafford
9. Meredith Willson and Orchestra
10. Max Terr Chorus

MAXWELL HOUSE
JANUARY 5, 1939

Page

1-1A.	OPENING
	BAND – "HIGH FLYING"
2-2D.	YOUNG – DOUGLAS – WILLSON
2E.	MACPHAIL – "FUNNY OLD HILLS"
3-3F.	BABY SNOOKS
4-4A.	COMMERCIAL
5.	BAND – "THE MOTH"
6-6F.	MORGAN
7.	STATION BREAK
8.	BAND – "AMERICA CALLING"

9-9A.	SNOOKS POEM – BRICE – STAFFORD – YOUNG – WILLSON
10.	INTRO TO DRAMA – BRUCE – DOUGLAS – YOUNG – STAFFORD – BRICE
10A-10L.	DRAMA – "A ROSE BY ANY NAME" – DOUGLAS – BRUCE
11.	CONCERT HALL – MACPHAIL & CHORUS – "THE LOST CHORD"
12.	MORGAN – BRUCE – YOUNG – DOUGLAS
13-13A.	COMMERCIAL
14-14A.	FINALE – ENTIRE COMPANY – "SO HELP ME"
15.	CLOSING

HULL: Maxwell House Coffee presents…Good News of 1939!

MUSIC: MUSIC IN AND FADE

HULL: The makers of Maxwell House Coffee welcome you to another hour of entertainment from Metro-Goldwyn-Mayer Studios in Hollywood—and here is your host for this evening—Robert Young! (APPLAUSE)

YOUNG: Thank you, Warren. Good evening, everybody. We have a wonderful program for you tonight, with all the regular gang—Fanny Brice, Hanley the Stafford, Frankie the Morg, Meredith the Maestro—and two swell guests, Melvyn Douglas and Virginia Bruce. I ran into Mel in the Studio Commissary the other day, and we got to talking about the program, and he had a lot of interesting ideas about it, so I asked him to drop in tonight. He was very definite in some of his suggestions, so don't be surprised if he gives us quite a going over—in a nice way.

Now, Virginia Bruce was going to appear with me in a little lovemaking dramatic sketch, but I'd forgotten it was customary for the host to step aside in favor of his guests—so Mel Douglas will play the part. Am I sorry I asked *him*!

But at least I can make trouble for somebody. Meredith Willson wants to start our first 1939 program with a new song that he thinks will shortly be a hit. I think I'll be able to slow it up a little, however, by being the first man to sing it on the air. So lift your hickory stickory, Meredy—and I will set forth the lyric.

MUSIC: YOUNG AND ORCHESTRA—"HIGH FLYIN'" (APPLAUSE)

YOUNG: Ladies and gentlemen, that applause was not for my singing, but for my friend Melvyn Douglas, who just walked in. How are you, Mel?

DOUGLAS: Fine, Bob. And I thought you sang very nicely.

YOUNG: Well, that just goes to show. You'd think that if a guy wanted to make some suggestions about the program, my singing would be a good place to start.

DOUGLAS: Now, just a minute, Robert. You seem to be suffering from the delusion that I think there's something the matter with the Good News Program. I like the program. It's fine—but I think it lacks one thing.

YOUNG: All right—what?

DOUGLAS: You have an audience of millions. What a chance to accomplish something of value—to get over a message of real and lasting interest—

YOUNG: We do.

DOUGLAS: Really? It must have eluded me. What's the message, Bob?

YOUNG: Maxwell House coffee is good to the last drop.

DOUGLAS: (LAUGHS) That's an important message—but my dear fellow, everyone *knows* that Maxwell House is good to the last drop! Besides—that's the message that stimulates the appetite, not the mind. But think how marvelous it would be if every Thursday, as soon as your program is over, twenty million people are all thinking—HARD—about something you have told them.

YOUNG: How do you know they're not?

DOUGLAS: I know very well what they're thinking. They're thinking, "Now it's time for Bing Crosby."

YOUNG: That's right. All right, Mel, what do you think we ought to do about it?

DOUGLAS: Give your listeners something valuable—something of permanent interest, something that will enrich their lives. Take Einstein, for instance.

YOUNG: Albert Einstein.

DOUGLAS: Yes. He created the Theory of Relativity. He's undoubtedly the greatest man alive in the world today. His name and face are as familiar to newspaper readers as the name and face of anybody, except possibly Seabiscuit—but if you listen to the big variety programs on the radio, what do you hear about Einstein?

YOUNG: Not much, I'll admit.

DOUGLAS: You hear just one thing. Somebody says, "I saw Albert Einstein last week," and another fellow says, "How did you find him?" And the first fellow says, "I just pushed back his hair, and there he was."

YOUNG: Well, Mel, you see there's where the Good News program is different. We used that joke, but we told it about Meredith Willson.

DOUGLAS: I can see how you might be tempted. (That's really a magnificent mane, isn't it?) However—that does not alter the fact that on the Good News program you have not honored the greatest physicist of the 20th Century—a man whose mind has revolutionized all our thinking about the world we live in. The Theory of Relativity is something every intelligent person should understand thoroughly! In fact—

YOUNG: Now wait a minute, Mel—I've been told there are only ten people in the world that understand Relativity.

DOUGLAS: Absurd! Any educated person can comprehend it readily—why not explain it on the radio?

YOUNG: Mel, I think you're right. And I tell you what we'll do.

DOUGLAS: What?

YOUNG: I'll let you explain the Theory of Relativity now. Go ahead.

DOUGLAS: No, Bob—I don't think I'd better.

YOUNG: Why not?

DOUGLAS: For a number of reasons. In the first place, I don't know anything about relativity—

YOUNG: I think you can let the others go. Melvyn, you've disappointed our listeners.

DOUGLAS: Do you really think so?

YOUNG: I'm sure of it. Think of the millions of people who've just been sitting on the edge of their chairs waiting to hear Melvyn Douglas, an actor, talk about relativity—

DOUGLAS: And I've let them down. I'm terribly sorry. Well, perhaps I chose an unfortunate example.

YOUNG: How do you mean?

DOUGLAS: I mean the subject doesn't matter, as long as it's really worthwhile. History, sociology, art—what about modern art?

YOUNG: Well, what about it? I'm all for it.

DOUGLAS: So am I. So is everybody. But do you tell your listeners anything about modern art? Think of the poor devils! Sitting at home drinking highballs while the radio plays swing music—when they could be enjoying a five-minute talk on The Significance of Picasso and Impressionism in Modern Art.

YOUNG: Tsk, tsk. Could that be covered in five minutes?

DOUGLAS: Oh, very easily!

YOUNG: Well, why don't you—

DOUGLAS: (CUTS HIM SHORT) But not by Melvyn Douglas. Possibly you won't believe this, Bob, but it happens that the subject of Picasso is another of the wide open spaces in my mind.

YOUNG: You picked out both subjects.

DOUGLAS: That's because I'm more the subject-selecting type than the information-giving type. It's the fault of the radio for not educating me.

YOUNG: Melvyn, that's the last straw. You owe our audience a little uplifting, and you've got to come through. Give out a three-minute talk on—Ibsen.

DOUGLAS: Now don't bully me. There are other contributions besides lectures, Robert. Another deficiency I have observed in your program, for example, is a shortage of instrumental music.

YOUNG: A shortage? With those 32 lugs in Willson's band?

DOUGLAS: Shh! They have feelings! Besides, I mean solo work. What famous pianists have you presented? Or cellists?

YOUNG: Bob Taylor.

DOUGLAS: Any performers on the lute? The lyre?

YOUNG: Frank Morgan.

DOUGLAS: What of the harpsichord, the thrumbole, the spinet? Not one.

YOUNG: All right, Melvyn—give out a couple of licks on the spinet.

DOUGLAS: I don't play the spinet—but it happens I have devoted many years of practice on an instrument which in many ways is closer to the soul of man that any other. An instrument which combines the sweetness of the flute, the sonority of the cello, the nobility of the violin—and the mobility of the vest pocket cigarette lighter. I am a virtuoso on the mouth organ.

YOUNG: Well, now we're getting somewhere. Ladies and gentlemen, Melvyn Douglas will bring you culture on his mouth organ. I imagine it will be at least a Bach fugue—am I right, Melvyn?

DOUGLAS:	The contrapuntal style is not suitable for the mouth organ, Robert—at least not for the Douglas mouth organ. I propose to play a beautiful American classic—"Swanee River." Incidentally, it sounds a lot better if I get a good loud accompaniment.
YOUNG:	All right. Meredith, will you get together with Melvyn Douglas on Swanee River in the key of —
DOUGLAS:	The key of G, please.
MEREDITH:	Right-o. Whenever you're ready, Mr. Douglas.
MUSIC:	DOUGLAS AND WILLSON—SWANEE RIVER (APPLAUSE)
YOUNG:	Ladies and gentlemen, you have just heard forty seconds of uplift from Melvyn Douglas and his mouth organ. Now, with his kind permission, we return to the field of popular entertainment. Douglas MacPhail, our Good News baritone, will sing. What's the song, Meredith?
MEREDITH:	Oh, it's very good, Bob. It's a cowboy song—a song sung by a lonesome cowboy who has nobody to sing to except Frank Morgan and his brother.
YOUNG:	A song to Frank Morgan and his brother? What's the name of it?
MEREDITH:	Those Funny Old Heels.
SOUND:	PROP LAUGH
YOUNG:	I don't know, maybe the culture was better. Go ahead, Douglas MacPhail—and sing the new Bing Crosby hit, "Funny Old Hills."
MUSIC:	MACPHAIL & ORCHESTRA - FUNNY OLD HILLS (APPLAUSE)
YOUNG:	(WHILE APPLAUSE IS STILL GOING ON) That was swell, Doug!
MACPHAIL:	Thank you, Bob.
YOUNG:	Mr. MacPhail will be back with us later—but at the moment we return to the uplift department—or possibly I should say culture. Anyway, here is Fanny Brice as Baby Snooks!
MUSIC:	(APPLAUSE)
YOUNG:	For many years, Daddy, played by Hanley Stafford, has been a physical culture fiend. It is very early in the morning as we find him dressed in his gym clothes doing his setting up exercises…Listen.
FATHER:	One - two - three - four! Hands on hips—inhale! (INHALES) Ahhhhhhhhhhhhhh! Boy, does that make you feel good!…Let's have a look at myself in the mirror…Hmmmmm! Guess the old boy's still got a pretty good physique. Yessir, pretty good!

BRICE:	Hello, Daddy.
FATHER:	(CHEERFULLY) Good morning, Snooks. What brings my little darling out of bed so early on this bright and sunny morning?
BRICE:	Huh?
FATHER:	How about a nice big kiss for daddy?
BRICE:	Do you feel alright, Daddy?
FATHER:	Never felt better in my life!
BRICE:	Why are you wearing that funny underwear?
FATHER:	That's not underwear. That's the way I dress for gym.
BRICE:	Jim who?
FATHER:	I'm talking about gymnasium.
BRICE:	Jim whosium?
FATHER:	Gymnasium!
BRICE:	Who's he?
FATHER:	It's not a he!
BRICE:	Is it a she?
FATHER:	Oh - what's the difference!
BRICE:	You gonna let her see you in your underwear?
FATHER:	Snooks - this is not my underwear and I am not going to let anyone see me!
BRICE:	Why?
FATHER:	Because the kind of gym I'm talking about is spelled g-y-m and the other Jim is J-i-m and one is gym and the other is Jim and neither one has anything to do with the other!
BRICE:	Are you sure you feel all right, Daddy?
FATHER:	Snooks, you can't make me mad this morning! I feel too good.
BRICE:	Why?
FATHER:	It's this morning workout! Would you believe I came into the house at four o'clock this morning, and—
BRICE:	Where was you so late, Daddy?
FATHER:	Er - I - er - I had to go sit up with a sick friend. Yes, a sick friend! (CLUCKS SYMPATHETICALLY)

BRICE: (DOES THE SAME)

FATHER: Anyway—all I got was two hours of sleep and I still feel great. You know why?

BRICE: Uh-huh - 'cause you won last night!

FATHER: Nothing of the kind—I lost! I mean—er—I didn't play! Now listen here, Snooks—please don't try to upset me this morning.

BRICE: Awight, Daddy.

FATHER: Move out of my way...Now! Hands on hips! Left foot forward! Dip! Right foot forward! Dip! Left—

BRICE: Can I dance with you, Daddy?

FATHER: I'm not dancing! I'm doing setting-up exercises—and I've been doing them every day for two years.

BRICE: Why?

FATHER: To build me up. Two years ago I was nothing but a flabby mess of soft, shapeless, ugly flesh. Now look at the change!

BRICE: What change?

FATHER: Oh! That's very funny—you're a scream—I'm splitting my sides with laughter (NASTY, MEAN LAUGH)

BRICE: (LAUGHS)

FATHER: (ANGRY) What are you laughing at?

BRICE: You split your underwear, too!

FATHER: IT'S NOT MY UNDERWEAR!

BRICE: Then whose is it?

FATHER: These are clothes I bought for gym!

BRICE: Then why doesn't Jim wear them?

FATHER: JIM WHO?

BRICE: I dunno!

FATHER: (HOARSELY CONTROLLING HIMSELF) Listen, Snooks—I woke up feeling great this morning—I didn't have a care in my mind—I didn't send for you—you walked in here and now I'm practically a nervous wreck—thanks to you!

BRICE: You're welcome, Daddy.

FATHER: Ahhh—what's the use! Hands on hips—left foot forward—bend the trunk—

BRICE: Daddy!

FATHER: What is it?

BRICE: I'm a naughty girl, ain't I?

FATHER: (MAD) Hmmmm! You can say that again!

BRICE: I'm a naughty girl, ain't I?

FATHER: What are you doing?

BRICE: You told me to say it again.

FATHER: Oh, never mind. Go back to bed and let me finish my exercises. I've got to take off a couple of pounds. (MUTTERS) Guess I have got a bit of a bay window at that.

BRICE: Huh?

FATHER: Nothing! I'm just angry because you made those nasty remarks about my—my figure! AND I DON'T LIKE IT—YOU UNDERSTAND!

BRICE: Why?

FATHER: BECAUSE I DON'T! (CONCERNED) Is my shape really that bad, Snooks?

BRICE: I think it's very pretty, Daddy.

FATHER: Now you're talking! (LAUGHS) I knew you were only fooling - yes sir! (LAUGHS)

BRICE: (LAUGHS)

FATHER: Just feel this muscle in my arm, Snooks—it's like iron!

BRICE: Ooooh—I like it!

FATHER: Bet I'd be a killer in the ring! I'm muscle all over.

BRICE: You've got a awful big muscle in your tummy. It's like jelly!

FATHER: Huh? Mmm—that darn pot! Gotta get that down. Give me that medicine ball…(GRUNTS)

BRICE: Why are you laying on the ball, Daddy?

FATHER: (GRUNTS) Gotta reduce my stomach.

BRICE: Why?

FATHER: It's too big.

BRICE: Will that make your tummy small?

FATHER: I don't know. I may have to diet.

BRICE: Huh?

FATHER:	I said I may have to diet.	
BRICE:	What color is it now?	
FATHER:	It's no color at all, silly!	
BRICE:	Make it green, Daddy!	
FATHER:	Will you stop that nonsense! My stomach's the same color as everybody's and it's going to stay that way!	
BRICE:	Is it the same color as mine?	
FATHER:	Of course.	
BRICE:	Is it the same color as my teacher's?	
FATHER:	YES!	
BRICE:	Has my teacher got a green stomach?	
FATHER:	NO!	
BRICE:	Who told you, Daddy?	
FATHER:	Nobody told me! Nobody has a green stomach!	
BRICE:	Frogs has a green stomach!	
FATHER:	Well, I'm not a frog!	
BRICE:	Why?	
FATHER:	Oh, leave me alone! You're going right back to bed, young lady!	
BRICE:	I ain't.	
FATHER:	(COYLY) Oh, yes you are!	
BRICE:	Oh, no I ain't!	
FATHER:	Well, will you keep quiet for two minutes so I can do my breathing exercises?	
BRICE:	I wanna do it, too.	
FATHER:	Oh, all right. Stand near this open window, take a deep breath and throw your chest out.	
BRICE:	Huh?	
FATHER:	Throw your chest out!	
BRICE:	Out the window?	
FATHER:	No! No! Fill your lungs with fresh air and your chest will expand…like this…inhale! (THEY BOTH DO) Exhale! (THEY DO) Inhale! Exhale!	

BRICE:	Waaaaahhhh!
FATHER:	What's the matter?
BRICE:	I'm getting dizzy.
FATHER:	That's on account of the oxygen. You'll get used to it if you take more rapid breaths. Breathe like a dog pants, Snooks—in very short breaths.
BRICE:	Awight.
FATHER:	Ready! (THEY BOTH BREATHE RAPIDLY FOR A COUPLE OF SECONDS) Don't stop, Snooks. Are you keeping up your short pants?
BRICE:	Uh-huh—but yours is coming down!
FATHER:	Nonsense! When I take a deep breath I expand my chest, raise my diaphragm and pull in my stomach. That's how to make muscles…You see, I—SNOOKS!
BRICE:	What's this thing?
FATHER:	Give it to me! That's a rubber muscle developer!
BRICE:	Huh?
FATHER:	It makes muscles. Give me the other end of it!
BRICE:	Wheee! It stretches!
FATHER:	SNOOKS!
BRICE:	Wheeeee! (LAUGHS)
FATHER:	Let go of that end! Look out! (TERRIFIC SMACK) Owwww! You let it fly right in my face! Ohhhh!
BRICE:	You told me to let go, Daddy.
FATHER:	Ohhhh! My eye! Look at it - it's swelling up like a balloon!
BRICE:	(LAUGHS)
FATHER:	WHAT ARE YOU LAUGHING AT!
BRICE:	It made a big muscle on your eye! (LAUGHS)
FATHER:	Yeah? Well, I'll make you such a muscle you won't sit down for a week! (SLAP—WILD LAUGH)
BRICE:	WAAAAHHHHH!
MUSIC:	(APPLAUSE)

15

FIRST HALF OF SHOW

YOUNG: Warren, it's coffee time right now, and I don't want to steal your thunder, but there's something I've been wanting to say to everybody for quite a while now.

HULL: Sure, Bob. Go right ahead.

YOUNG: It's just this: this program has always been a favorite of mine. And when I made my first appearance on it some months ago, Betty—that's Mrs. Young—and I, quite naturally, made a point of trying Maxwell House Coffee.

Well, I thought you might be interested to know that we've used it ever since. Not that I'm any expert, but I *like* this new Maxwell House better than any coffee I've ever tried. All right, Warren?

HULL: Thanks, Bob. That was nice of you. We appreciate it. Friends, more and more people every day are saying things like that about the *new* Maxwell House Coffee. More people, in fact, are buying Maxwell House today than ever before in its history.

If *you* haven't tried Maxwell House lately, then we believe you're missing a rare treat in coffee goodness and satisfaction!

Ever since it was created—more than half a century ago—in Nashville, Tennessee, the Maxwell House blend has been known as one of the world's finest coffees.

Today, after months of effort and experimentation, we can announce that this famous blend is richer, more delicious, more full-bodied than ever before. You'll taste its extra richness in your very first steaming, fragrant cup.

Then, too, you'll appreciate the remarkable new radiant roast process, which, by roasting each coffee bean evenly, *all the way through*, brings out the true, natural flavor of the superb blend. No chance of bitter coffee due to parching, or weak coffee due to under-roasting.

The new Maxwell House comes to you in the same familiar blue super-vacuum can, with all its flavor and fragrance *sealed in*, none wasted.

So try a pound tomorrow, won't you? We think you'll say, "This is the finest coffee I've ever tasted." We think you'll agree that this new Maxwell House is more than ever…good to the last drop!

MUSIC: BRIDGE

YOUNG:	Leaving kidding aside for the moment, Meredith Willson is starting a new series tonight which really has a worthy aim. For many years it has been difficult for American composers of other than popular songs to get a hearing for their work. Often such works have even been published, only to gather dust on the shelves of music stores and publishers' warehouses, but never reaching the public ear. Meredith proposes to rescue some of the Underprivileged Masterpieces from time to time, in order to give them a chance for the popular favor he feels they deserve. In order to narrow the field, he is going to present only compositions of a descriptive character, or musical impressions. To inaugurate the series, Meredith has chosen a brilliant composition by the pianist Lee Sims called, "The Moth." Meredith—
MUSIC:	MEREDITH WILLSON AND ORCHESTRA - THE MOTH (APPLAUSE)

MORGAN-YOUNG-WILLSON SPOT

YOUNG:	Congratulations to Lee Sims—and thanks to Meredith Willson for allowing us to hear Mr. Sims' composition.
MEREDITH:	Did you really like it, Bob?
YOUNG:	Certainly.
MEREDITH:	I have another contribution I could make—sort of a cultural thing.
YOUNG:	Well now, Meredith, we don't want to go overboard on this. What is it you want to do?
MEREDITH:	I have a new impersonation of a famous radio star.
YOUNG:	No. Don't do it.
MEREDITH:	I'll bet anything you'd recognize it right away.
YOUNG:	Can't have it.
MEREDITH:	Please, Bob. It's 1939, you know.
YOUNG:	That has nothing to do with it!
MEREDITH:	Awwwwww—
YOUNG:	Will it take long?
MEREDITH:	Not a second. Here it is. Hiya, Buck!...Well, howdya like it?
YOUNG:	Fine.
DOUGLAS:	I thought it was divine.
YOUNG:	Oh—divine, huh? That's a big-time culture joke.

DOUGLAS: Don't go away, Meredith!

MEREDITH: Oh, I wasn't!

DOUGLAS: Meredith, I've been listening to you all evening, and I think there's something Shavian about you.

YOUNG: Shavian my foot! He don't even get a haircut!

MEREDITH: (VERY DIGNIFIED) A barnyard witticism, from an over-dressed ostler.

DOUGLAS: Very nicely put, Meredith! No one could have said that except an admirer of George Bernard Shaw.

YOUNG: Oh, Shaw, Shaw.

MEREDITH: Pardon, Mel?

DOUGLAS: I said I could see you've spent many happy hours with—G.B.S.

MEREDITH: Oh, no. I'm exclusive with NBC.

DOUGLAS: I'm afraid I've misjudged you. Haven't you seen Pygmalion?

YOUNG: No, he doesn't like animal pictures.

MEREDITH: I do, too! Where is it playing?

YOUNG: Meredith, go away!

MEREDITH: Oh, sure! (HE GOES)

DOUGLAS: Well, Bob, you saw Pygmalion, didn't you?

YOUNG: I haven't had a chance. I mean to go this week, though.

DOUGLAS: You'll like it. Leslie Howard is marvelous as the professor of phonetics. Remember that wonderful bit, in the play, when he guesses where all the people came from, just by listening carefully to their speech?

YOUNG: Oh, sure! Of course that's something Shaw cooked up in his own mind. Nobody could possibly detect where a person comes from by the way he talks!

MORGAN: (COMING IN) Who said that? (NO APPLAUSE)

DOUGLAS: Oh, hello, Frank.

MORGAN: Hello, Mel! Say, Bob, which one of you untravelled illiterates was it who made the remark about not being able to detect a person's origin from his speech?

YOUNG: I did, teacher, go jump in the lake!

MORGAN: A Pomona boy.

DOUGLAS: Are you a student of phonetics, Frank?

MORGAN: A student? Son, would you call Rembrandt a student of painting? Would you call Einstein a student of physics? Would you call Hempstead two three hundred and see if Gladys is there? (Confound it! Who's been making free with my papers?)

YOUNG: Take it easy, Frank, nobody will remember it tomorrow!

MORGAN: They won't! Look at those musical scavengers! They're writing down her number now! I don't know why I come here—never in all my life have I known such a—

YOUNG: Frank! Pipe down!

DOUGLAS: I'm sorry I called you a student, Frank. Possibly I should have asked, "Are you a master of phonetics?"

MORGAN: That is one of my minor accomplishments. I am fluent in every language, every dialect, from ancient Sanskrit and Parsee through Swahili, Pictish, Coptic, and Esperanto.

YOUNG: Do you stop at Ypsilanti?

MORGAN: Change at Grand Rapids.

DOUGLAS: Track seven.

MORGAN: Board! But not only do I speak every language, gentlemen, I am the only man alive who has ever had a conversation with an anthropoid ape.

YOUNG: What are you looking at me for?

MORGAN: If the shoe fits, put it on. However, the ape I'm referring to wasn't even related to you, my boy. I conducted the experiment before a committee of four hundred eminent philologists, in the Persian Room at the British Museum.

DOUGLAS: What happened?

MORGAN: The gorilla was brought into the room in a cage—and my fellow scientists were aghast at my courage when I entered the huge animal's cell, alone and unarmed.

DOUGLAS: No precautions, Frank?

MORGAN: Certainly not! Melvyn, there is nothing difficult about making friends with an animal, even the most savage types, if you really have a feeling of affection toward him. I entered his cage with my arms outstretched, a smile on my face, and two keepers behind me with sawed-off shotguns…(GIGGLES)

YOUNG: No protection.

MORGAN: Er—no. The gorilla greeted me with a friendly snarl, and I answered him in kind.

YOUNG: I'll bet he understood that, Frank.

MORGAN: Not immediately. I hurled rapid fire questions at the ape in a variety of monkey dialects, but received no reply, while the four hundred philologists were scribbling like mad in their notebooks.

DOUGLAS: What kind of questions did you ask him, Frank?

MORGAN: I confined myself to questions likely to interest the monkey intelligence, such as conditions at the London Zoo, was he satisfied with his cage, the price of coconuts, and how was his wife and his four lovely baboons.

YOUNG: That should have got an answer.

MORGAN: I tried dialect after dialect—but nothing happened, until suddenly the gorilla began leaping up and down, like a monkey on a pogo stick, in a most terrifying manner. The scientists stiffened in their chairs, the guards tightened their grips on their gunstocks—and I widened my friendly smile. At this moment, I remembered an obscure Simian dialect I had picked up in the lobby of the Egyptian Theatre!

YOUNG: The Egyptian Theatre.

MORGAN: I hurled a question at the ape, and the response was instantaneous. Still bouncing up and down, he poured forth a torrent of monkey gibberish, starting with a small whine, and finishing with a double brandy and soda. (That's the last straw. The monkeys have been tampering with my notes!)

YOUNG: Keep swinging, Tarzan!

DOUGLAS: Frank, when the monkey began to talk, did you understand him?

MORGAN: An excellent question, Melvyn. The animal's language was definitely familiar—I recognized it as a jungle dialect called Schmutz, but there was something about his inflection that baffled me. Finally, I realized what it was!

YOUNG: What was it?

MORGAN: He'd been in the London Zoo so long he was talking Schmutz with a British accent!

DOUGLAS: Well, I don't suppose that bothered a cosmopolite like yourself.

MORGAN: Oh, far from it! Inside of ten minutes, we were jabbering away like old cronies. The scientists couldn't believe their ears, they were scribbling like mad with their pencils—but when the great ape finally got so friendly that he told me a famous jungle joke, the

	savants leaped from their chairs in their excitement, completely forgetting their nuts. I mean, their notes.
DOUGLAS:	What was this jungle joke, Frank?
MORGAN:	Just a little anecdote. As I recall, it was about a traveling salamander and a llama's daughter. (GIGGLES) Well, I gotta go, fellows. I have to see a man about a—
YOUNG:	Frank! You still haven't explained why the gorilla was jumping up and down.
MORGAN:	Err—jumping. Jumping. Did I say he was jumping?
DOUGLAS:	You said he was jumping up and down. Why?
MORGAN:	Er—why—gorilla—jumping. Er—yes! Well, I asked him about that at once, and he told me that just before the experiment he had taken his daily dose of monkey gland medicine, and had forgotten to shake the bottle. Well, I guess that takes care of the—
YOUNG:	Come here, Ape Man! There's still one link missing.
DOUGLAS:	Yes, Frank! When you first came in, you told us you could duplicate the feat in Pygmalion, and tell where a man came from by listening to his speech.
MORGAN:	Well, of course, Melvyn! That's child's play, but I haven't got time to play today, I—
YOUNG:	Make him prove it, Melvyn!
DOUGLAS:	Come on, Frank! Let's see a demonstration.
MORGAN:	All right, I'll tell you where Meredith comes from, if he —
YOUNG:	Oh, no! Get a stranger!
MORGAN:	Oh—Young—you have the tenacity of a bulldog, without his compensating beauty.
YOUNG:	(BARKS)
DOUGLAS:	Why not get someone from the audience, Frank?
MORGAN:	It's a conspiracy! All right—er—you there—the young fellow in the front row—would you mind stepping up on the stage, please?
YOUNG:	You better not strike out now, Pygmalion!
MORGAN:	Just step aside, Young. Just come right up here to the microphone, my boy.
BOY:	Yes, sir.
MORGAN:	That's fine. Now say something for me.

BOY:	What do you want me to say?
MORGAN:	That's enough. Gentlemen, this young man was born in Hartford, Connecticut, was educated in that city and in Westchester County, New York, and judging from your clipped vowels and overlaid consonants, I should say you had spent roughly eight years, four months, and twenty-three days in California. That's all.
DOUGLAS:	Wait a minute! Young man, is it possible he's right?
BOY:	He's absolutely right, sir.
MORGAN:	(LAUGHS TRIUMPHANTLY) Well, gentlemen, I hope you're—
YOUNG:	No you don't! There's something fishy about this! I'll bet he knows the kid!
MORGAN:	(HURT) Why, Young! You have the infernal impudence to stand there and make a bold-faced accusation like that! I suffer enough from your childish witticisms, but when you impugn my integrity—oh! I'll leave it to the boy. Young man, have you ever seen me before in your life?
BOY:	No, Dad.
MORGAN:	I've been stabbed! Get out of here! Wait 'til I get you home! (WALKS OFF CURSING HIS SON)
MUSIC:	PLAY OFF (APPLAUSE)

COMMERCIAL: STATION BREAK COMMERCIAL

YOUNG:	Well, Warren, there's a fragrance in the air that tells me it's time right now for that familiar Thursday evening custom of ours ...
DOUGLAS:	What custom is that, Bob?
YOUNG:	Hello, Melvyn. Why, it's our regular time out, for a moment of relaxation over a steaming, friendly cup of—
DOUGLAS:	Maxwell House Coffee? Excuse me for butting in, fellows, but that's a custom I observe every day in the year in my own home. So may I join you right now?
HULL:	You certainly may, Melvyn. And friends, we hope all of you listening in will, too. So pull up your chairs, one and all, and enjoy a freshly made cup of this coffee that's good to the last drop, while Meredith pipes us a tune…
MUSIC:	UP AND FADE
HULL:	We now pause briefly for station identification.
MUSIC:	UP AND FADE

YOUNG:	This is Bob Young again, and we continue our Good News Maxwell House Program with Virginia Bruce and Melvyn Douglas, who will appear in a few moments in a dramatic sketch - Baby Snooks, Frank Morgan, Douglas MacPhail, and Meredith Willson. Meredith is now going to rescue another somewhat Underprivileged Masterpiece—a march written by Meredith Willson three weeks ago. It was written especially for the program broadcast from Hollywood to celebrate the anniversary of the American Bill of Rights. If you heard the program, I'm sure you remember the march, entitled "America Calling."
MUSIC:	MEREDITH WILLSON & ORCHESTRA—AMERICA CALLING (APPLAUSE)
YOUNG:	Very good, Meredith. If that doesn't help the song, get a lyric for it, and I'll sing it.
MEREDITH:	Oh, thanks, Bob. Guess I'll save that as a kind of a—last resort, you might say.
YOUNG:	Pray do. And now, ladies and gentlemen—
HANLEY:	Excuse me, Bob.
YOUNG:	Hello, Hanley. How's that eye of yours?
HANLEY:	It's a little better, thank you. I—er—I came to ask you a favor.
YOUNG:	Yes?
HANLEY:	You know that poem that Snooks recited a couple of weeks ago—
YOUNG:	The Owl and the Pussycat? Yes.
HANLEY:	Well, she's been pestering me to let her—you know, the kid—
YOUNG:	Mm-hmm. Stage-struck, huh?
HANLEY:	(BRIDLING) What do you mean stage-struck! She can recite as well as your kid!
YOUNG:	All right, Daddy - don't lose your temper. We'll be very happy to let Snooks recite another poem. Bring her on!
HANLEY:	Thanks…oh, Snooks!
BRICE:	Yes, Daddy?
HANLEY:	Go ahead and recite.
BRICE:	Awrite…er—
HANLEY:	Give the title. Go on.
BRICE:	(THE THREE LITTLE KITTENS)

HANLEY:	Fine.
DOUGLAS:	Snooks, I think you did that beautifully!
SNOOKS:	Thank you, Mr. Douglas.
BRUCE:	Marvelous, Snooks! But I think your father deserves congratulations, too.
HANLEY:	Thank you, Miss Bruce. I guess the child inherits a bit of my talent.
BRUCE:	Oh, I'm sure she does!
YOUNG:	All right, thank you, Snooks, thank you, Daddy. Now, ladies and gentlemen, the MGM Theater of the Air presents Melvyn Douglas and Virginia Bruce, who may be seen together, by the way, in their new Columbia picture, "There's That Woman Again."
DOUGLAS:	I've been waiting for that.
YOUNG:	Quiet, uplifter! We present Miss Bruce and Mr. Douglas in a drama especially written for this program by Robert Riley Crutcher, and directed by Edgar Selwyn, Metro-Goldwyn-Mayer producer. The title is "A Rose by Any Name." Music, please, Meredith?
MUSIC:	MUSIC IN (DRAMA)

SECOND HALF OF SHOW

YOUNG:	Now here's Warren Hull, with some good news for everyone to whom a good cup of coffee is important. And that's just about everybody, Warren...
HULL:	Good news travels fast, and on every hand you hear more and more comments like these about the new, marvelously improved Maxwell House Coffee.
VOICE #1:	(MAN-SIMPLE-UNAFFECTED) Say, this is what I call coffee! Got a real richness and body to it.
SOUND:	CLINK OF CUP IN SAUCER
VOICE #1:	Let's stick to this *new* Maxwell House, Mary!
VOICE #2:	(WOMAN-ELDERLY-SOUTHERN) Maxwell House has been in my home for fifty years that I can remember—and today it's finer-tasting coffee than ever.
VOICE #3:	(WOMAN-YOUNG)...and send me two pounds of Maxwell House, Mr. Jones. Getting my money's worth means a lot to me, and I want to know the coffee *I* buy is *really* fresh!

HULL:	…really fresh coffee! One truly important reason why more people are enjoying the new Maxwell House than ever before.
	Unlike ordinary methods of packing coffee, which allow air to enter and steal away the flavor, Maxwell House is taken still fresh and fragrant from the roasting ovens and packed in an airtight, super-vacuum can. No air can get in—so no flavor can get out. All the fragrance and flavor of these superb coffees are sealed in for you—none wasted.
	Friend, for more than fifty years we've worked to make Maxwell House the finest coffee you can possibly buy. Today, with the marvelously enriched blend and new process of roasting, the *new* Maxwell House is more delicious, more downright satisfying than ever.
	And remember, next time you order the familiar blue can from your grocer, you are buying coffee not just days fresh, but *roaster-fresh*. And no coffee can be fresher than that!
MUSIC:	BRIDGE
HULL:	Next week, ladies and gentlemen, Good News will bring you a truly great show. Names that spell the finest in entertainment. Heading our guest list, sensational singing personality…the star of MGM's "Great Waltz"…Militza Korjus. And a special treat for the ladies… "If Men Went Apartment Hunting as Women Do." Back to thrill us with his grand voice—Tony Martin. And of course, Fanny Brice, Hanley Stafford, Frank Morgan, Dennis O'Keefe, Nat Pendleton, Allan Curtis, Cecelia Parker, Meredith Willson, and Bob Young.
YOUNG:	Nice advance billing, Warren. Well, ladies and gentlemen, that about ties up the loose ends on our little bundle of Good News for tonight, but before taking leave of you 'til Thursday, may I remind you to round up the family and take them to your favorite picture theatre to see Wallace Beery and Robert Taylor in "Stand Up and Fight," a Mervyn LeRoy production, directed by W.S. Van Dyke II. Take my word for it, they'll appreciate the treat. This is Bob Young, saying—"Goodnight."
MUSIC:	MUSIC IN
HULL:	This is Warren Hull saying goodnight and good luck from the makers of Maxwell House—the coffee that's always good to the last drop.
	This is the National Broadcasting Company.

MAXWELL HOUSE COFFEE TIME
JULY 3, 1941

1. SNOOKS AND DADDY
2. THEME AND CAST INTRO – "NIGHT WE MET IN HONOMU"
3. FRANK MORGAN SPOT
4. MIDDLE COMMERCIAL
5. "LA PALOMA"
6. BABY SNOOKS SPOT
7. CLOSING COMMERCIAL
8. "RELUCTANT DRAGON"
9. SIGN-OFF
10. HITCH-HIKE

BRICE: Daddy.

FATHER: What is it, Snooks?

BRICE: What's this book with pictures in it?

FATHER: Let's see. Hmm. That's an old family album. Haven't looked at that thing in ten years.

BRICE: Shall I burn it?

FATHER: No, of course not! You say that as though these pictures were something to be ashamed of.

BRICE: You better look at them, Daddy.

FATHER: I am looking, and I think they're fine. What's wrong with this old gentleman?

BRICE: He ain't got no face.

FATHER: Oh, stop it. It's true his forehead is a little low, but I think he looks quite distinguished. That's my Uncle Maxwell.

BRICE: Is he the one who used to be the bearded lady in the cir—

FATHER:	Snooks! He used to drive a horse-car in the old days.
BRICE:	Horse-car?
FATHER:	That's right. Many's the time I rode on old Uncle Maxwell's horse-car.
BRICE:	How much did it cost, Daddy?
FATHER:	I think the fee was a dime. Yes! Here's a dime glued above his picture.
BRICE:	I thought that was his hat.
FATHER:	What do you know about that. This is the first dime Uncle Maxwell ever took in as a fee on his horse-car. Isn't that wonderful?
BRICE:	Why?
FATHER:	Do you realize what that is!
BRICE:	No. What is it?
FATHER:	It's Maxwell horse-car-fee dime!
BRICE:	Ohhhh, Daddy!
MUSIC:	(APPLAUSE)
ANNOUNCER:	Yes, ladies and gentlemen, it doesn't take a brilliant mind to understand that Daddy meant it was Maxwell House Coffee Time, and once again to enjoy Frank Morgan, Hanley Stafford, Meredith Willson and his Orchestra, and the result of Fanny BRICE's mental aberrations—the one and only Baby Snooks!
BRICE:	I didn't do nothing.
AUDIENCE:	(APPLAUSE)
ANNOUNCER:	And here is our master of ceremonies, your host for the evening, John Conte!
MUSIC:	CONTE AND ORCHESTRA – THE NIGHT WE MET IN HONOMU
	(APPLAUSE)
CONTE:	Thank you, ladies and gentlemen, and good evening.
MAN:	(COMING ON) All right, fellers, set the cameras up right here. Where's Morgan, buddy?
CONTE:	Buddy? Who are you, mister?
MAN:	Max Forst, Metro Publicity Department. Where's Morgan?
CONTE:	Well, I'm sorry, Mr. Forst, but I don't know where Mr. Morgan is right at the—

MORGAN: (COMING ON) One more word from you, my man, and you'll hear from my solicitors!

CONTE: Frank! (APPLAUSE)

MORGAN: Hello, fellows! The colossal impudence of those musicians!

MEREDITH: What's this? What's this?

MAN: Hahzit, Frank! We're here with the cameras. How about a little shot?

MORGAN: All right—but go easy on the sodas, if you don't—oh! Camera shot! Certainly.

MEREDITH: Wait a minute—what's this about my musicians?

MORGAN: Oh, hell, Meredith. I was just paying off a little baseball bet, and your harpist gave me an argument that gold wasn't legal tender.

MAN: Hey, Frank, will you turn around a bit?

CONTE: Hold on there, Mr. Forst, I want to talk to Mr. Morgan for a minute.

MAN: Okay. (MUTTERS) Broken down radio actors.

MORGAN: What's that?

CONTE: Never mind him, Frank. What's this about paying off a bet to the harpist?

MORGAN: If he keeps insisting that gold isn't legal tender I won't pay him!

MEREDITH: Did you offer him gold, Frank?

MORGAN: Better than that! I offered him two shares in the P&M Goldmine! The opportunity of his life, and he turned it down!

CONTE: Is this goldmine any good, Frank?

MORGAN: Any good? It's practically a goldmine! Why if I—

CONTE: Is there any gold in it?

MORGAN: Are you serious, Comet? The mother lode is pure forty-eight carat gold!

CONTE: Forty-eight carat!

MORGAN: Certainly! I had the assay office check—

CONTE: Frank! How can you stand there and say the mother lode is forty-eight carat gold when everybody knows it doesn't go higher than twenty-four!

MORGAN: Errr—twenty-four. Yes. Well, this mother lode had twins! (GIGGLES) All right, fellows, you can take your pictures now.

MAN:	Okay, Frank. Give us your best angle, kid. Grab that, fellows!
MORGAN:	Are you done now?
MAN:	Just a couple more. How about a comedy shot?
MORGAN:	Comedy shot?
MAN:	You know. Full face.
MORGAN:	Oh, full face. Young man, may I say I think you're extremely offensive, even for a press agent?
MAN:	That's me, Frank—most offensive guy in town. But you can't say I don't deliver. Last year I had you in the public eye, this year I got you in the public heart—no telling where you'll be next year!
MORGAN:	I have a vague idea, but don't go too far south! I wish you'd hurry and get through with your pictures, I'm getting nervous.
MAN:	All done now, Frank. So long, kid. (HE BLOWS) Come on, boys.
MEREDITH:	What's all the pictures for, Frank?
MORGAN:	Just some advance releases on my new picture, Honkytonk.
CONTE:	*Your* new picture? Who else is in the cast?
MORGAN:	Err—cast. I have a list here somewhere—oh, here. Here it is.
CONTE:	Agnes, Mabel, Irene—Hollywood 244—
MORGAN:	Wrong list! Let's have that, Jockey.
MEREDITH:	Say, isn't Honkytonk the picture that stars Clark Gable and Lana Turner?
MORGAN:	Clark Turner...now that you mention it I believe I did see their names on the call sheet. A promising pair of lads, if they spare them in the cutting room.
CONTE:	You'd better watch your step, Frank. If Metro finds out you're making light of Clark Gable and Lana Turner there might be trouble.
MORGAN:	Nonsense! Everybody knows who gives the best performance in the picture, and I'm quite sure my work won't go unrewarded. Never have I striven to reach such a degree of perfection in playing a role—every morning at seven finds me hard at work getting into character!
CONTE:	What part do you play?
MORGAN:	A drunken judge. A curious bit of casting because I've never been a judge in my life. (Hmm...I'm beginning to see why they put a morals clause in my contract.)

MEREDITH: What's the picture about, Frank? Huh?

MORGAN: Well, I'm not at liberty to divulge the story, but most of the action takes place around a mining camp. Clark Gable is a cardsharp, and Lana Turner plays my daughter.

MEREDITH: Wow!

MORGAN: That's what I thought, too, Meredith, but she treats me the same way off set. Rather ungrateful, to say the least.

MEREDITH: Ungrateful? Why should a fine actress like Lana Turner be grateful to you, Frank?

MORGAN: Well, I'd hardly expect you to understand, Cobbler. You're not in pictures—and I can think of several reasons why—but it's customary for an actress to be grateful when she's given the breaks in all the camera angles.

MEREDITH: Gee, this is interesting. I wish I knew what that meant.

CONTE: Morgan's modestly trying to tell us that he allows Miss Turner to steal scenes from him. Isn't that right, Frank?

MORGAN: Nothing of the kind! I've merely pointed out to the director how to place the camera so that certain outstanding features that Miss Turner possesses may be brought into greater prominence.

MEREDITH: She sure has got beautiful eyes.

MORGAN: Yes. Only yesterday we were shooting a scene where Lana Turner is trapped in a mine cave-in—and I suggested that the camera be placed right among the falling debris to give the scene realism.

CONTE: It's been done a thousand times.

MORGAN: Not the way I wanted it. My idea was to have bits of flying rock actually hit the lens of the camera, and a shower of fragments completely envelop everything for a climax. And that's the way they shot it!

MEREDITH: Jeepers! You'd think that would break the lens!

MORGAN: It did. And the camera—and the director's arm. Fortunately, I was able to repair the instrument before any great production loss was sustained, and the picture contin—

CONTE: Frank! You say you repaired the camera?

MORGAN: After I set the director's arm, yes.

CONTE: Do you understand the mechanism of those things?

MORGAN: (LAUGHS IMMODERATELY) Oh, come, my dear boy—you must be jesting!

CONTE: I'm not jesting! Do you understand the mechanism of a motion picture camera?

MORGAN: Would you have the temerity to ask Alexander Graham Bell if he understood the mechanism of the telephone?

CONTE: No—but Bell *invented* the telephone!

MORGAN: Well?

CONTE: Oh, no! Now, look here—you're not going to give off that you invented the movie camera, Mr. Morgan!

MORGAN: Screeno Morgan, sir! For generations the Morgans have dabbled in pictures, and I'm the last of a long line of postcards! I've been framed!

MEREDITH: Say, do you fellows know the average rainfall in Mason City is around fourteen and three tenths inches a year?

MORGAN: What?

CONTE: What's that got to do with motion pictures, Meredith?

MEREDITH: Oh, nothing—but I haven't said anything for five minutes and I'd like to get in on the conversation.

MORGAN: Well, this is becoming intolerable. I'm not going to hang aroun—

CONTE: Don't' go, Frank. I'd like to hear how you came to invent the motion picture camera.

MORGAN: Well, all right. It all started when my uncle, Double Feature Morgan, conceived the idea that pictures might be made to move. If it hadn't been for his wife, Aunt Sprocket, he might never have tried his experiment.

MEREDITH: What did she do?

MORGAN: Well, she encouraged him in shorts. His first attempt was a miserable failure and that was all the spur I needed to make me carry on. I needn't tell you that I carried on plenty before I was twenty-one, and soon made a name for myself as black sheep of the family. (This is getting a little wild, isn't it?)

MEREDITH: Sure, but I love it. Go on, Frank.

MORGAN: Yes. Well, I set up a small laboratory in 1854—

CONTE: 1854!

MORGAN: 1854 Grumble Street, the Bronx. That's right at the corner of Surly Street. The year was 1902—and I worked with the frenzy and determination of youth. By 1903 I made pictures move, by 1906 I made them talk, and some day I hope to make them smell!

(SHAKES HIS HEAD)

CONTE: Frank! What are you saying?

MEREDITH: Keep quiet, John! If he says he'll make pictures smell, he'll do it! Go on, Frank!

MORGAN: I can see Meredith is aware that I'm referring to projecting pleasant aromas from the screen, to accompany floral scenes—an impossible task, even for me.

CONTE: Well, where did you learn all about photography, Frank?

MORGAN: While I was still an apple-cheeked schoolboy I mastered the chemistry of light emulsions, and also became familiar with the peephole principle. In those days I was known as Tom.

CONTE: Go on, Tom.

MORGAN: As I said before, I constructed my first movie camera in 1903—a crude instrument compared with those in use today—but miraculous when you consider that I made it entirely from odds and ends which I purchased at no expense from a junk shop.

CONTE: Did it work?

MORGAN: Well, all I can tell you is that even before I had it completed, the Smithsonian Institution sat with bated breath waiting for the final result. Gentlemen, I don't have to tell you where that first Morgan Camera reposes today.

MEREDITH: In the Smithsonian Institution!

MORGAN: No, it's in the junk shop. My second attempt bore fruit, however, the camera worked like a charm, and I was ready to shoot the first motion picture. I dashed off a screen story and engaged an enormous cast of capable actors, including a leading lady who was three-fourths Indian and one-fourth Caledonian.

MEREDITH: One-fourth Scotch? What's that?

MORGAN: A quarter Scotch.

MEREDITH: I'll have a pint of rye.

MORGAN: Any Shasta?

MEREDITH: Two bottles, please.

MORGAN: That'll be four doll—what are we talking about!

CONTE: You cut that out, Meredith! Go on, Frank!

MORGAN: Yes. I'll look into that bit of by-play later!

MEREDITH: I'm sorry, Frank. I just lost myself in your story. Please tell us what happened when you got ready to shoot your picture.

MORGAN: Well, everything was in complete readiness, actors rehearsed, camera set up, lights in position—and then I remembered! I was aghast!

CONTE: What did you remember, Frank?

MORGAN: No one had invented film!

MEREDITH: You need that, don't you?

MORGAN: It was up to me again. I knew that snapshot film was made with celluloid, but how was a poor inventor to come by five hundred feet of it with which to make a motion picture? I racked my brains for days, and finally hit the solution.

CONTE: You bought it from Eastman.

MORGAN: No! But had you been in the vicinity of Mott and Pell Streets, New York's Chinatown, that fateful night in 1903, you might have seen a tall, distinguished inventor darting in and out of Chinese laundries, carrying mysterious bundles.

MEREDITH: It was you, Frank!

MORGAN: Yes!

CONTE: What have you got in the bundles, Frank?

MORGAN: Celluloid collars, my boy! Thousands of them! I rushed them to my lab, and with infinite patience I coated each one with emulsion, spliced them carefully and pierced the sprockets by hand. Three nights later I previewed the first motion picture ever made at the Old Madison Square Garden, and was cheered by an audience of bluebloods, red-bloods, and a few anemics. The Academy of Arts awarded—

CONTE: Frank! Now wait a minute!

MORGAN: What?

CONTE: What kind of a picture could you make out of laundry?

MORGAN: Techni-collar! (GIGGLES) So long, boys—I'm gonna go see a newsreel.

MUSIC: (APPLAUSE)

COMMERCIAL

INTRO: MUSIC FROM ERA OF SPANISH-AMERICAN WAR, FADING AFTER A FEW BARS AS BACKGROUND FOR:

CONTE:	At 9:34 A.M.—just forty-three years ago today—the battleship Iowa signaled to the waiting American fleet—
MAN:	The enemy is attempting to escape!
CONTE:	The Spanish Fleet rushed, full steam, from the harbor of Santiago and the American Men-of-war gave chase, destroying in three and a half hours every one of the Spanish vessels. Commanding the Flagship Brooklyn in this great naval victory—called the Battle of Santiago—was Commodore Winfield Scott Schley.

COMMERCIAL: MIDDLE—263 WORDS—1 MINUTE 30 SECONDS

CONTE:	After the war ended, Commodore Schley's rank was raised to that of Admiral—and, in nineteen hundred and two, Admiral and Mrs. Schley were honored guests at the Maxwell House in Nashville, Tennessee. Theirs were among the hundreds of famous names on the Maxwell House register—statesmen, ambassadors, noted figures from the stage and opera—all entertained at this distinguished old hotel. For the Maxwell House was known far and wide for its hospitality, its rich cuisine, and also for—
SOUTHERN LADY:	(SLIGHT SOUTHERN ACCENT) I declare, doesn't the Maxwell House serve the most delicious coffee you ever tasted?
SOUTHERN GENTLEMAN:	(SLIGHT SOUTHERN ACCENT) It surely does, ma'am! I'm going to tell them down home this is the richest coffee I've ever had!
CONTE:	As the years rolled by, the fame of Maxwell House Coffee...the story of its rare and mellow flavor...spread far and wide throughout America. This year, more people are enjoying Maxwell House than ever before in its history. Truly, it has won the favor of the world's greatest nation of coffee lovers!
ANNOUNCER:	And no wonder, because today, the famous Maxwell House blend is richer than ever—wonderfully enriched with an extra measure of extra flavor coffees, from the highland plantations of Central and South America—coffees that add to every cup of Maxwell House, a deeper satisfaction—and a rarer pleasure for you!
	So, how about it? How about discovering this luxury of coffee goodness that everyone can afford to enjoy, and no one can afford to miss!
	If you're a coffee lover, you deserve Maxwell House...the coffee that's now...more than ever...good to the last drop!
CONTE:	That was very beautiful, Meredith. And now, ladies and gentle—

STAFFORD:	Hello, John.
CONTE:	Hello, Daddy. You look completely worn out!
STAFFORD:	And well I might be. Uncle Louie got married last week in Washington, and I made the trip to be best man.
CONTE:	Don't tell me you had to take—
STAFFORD:	She came along—just for the ride! It was frightful. We had to take a very late plane, and we arrived at the airport some time after midnight. I tried to keep Snooks occupied until—(FADES) the plane came in—
MUSIC:	SNOOKS PLAY-ON
FATHER:	Snooks! Get up off the floor! Your clothes'll be filthy before we get on the plane!
BRICE:	Where's the plane, Daddy?
FATHER:	It'll be here soon.
BRICE:	Where are we going?
FATHER:	I told you fifty times. We're going to Washington!
BRICE:	Why?
FATHER:	Because Uncle Louie's getting married and I'm going to be the best man at the wedding.
BRICE:	Well, what's Uncle Louie gonna be?
FATHER:	Hooked.
BRICE:	Huh?
FATHER:	Nothing. Get up off the floor.
BRICE:	Is Uncle Louie your uncle, Daddy?
FATHER:	No, he's your uncle. He's my half-brother.
BRICE:	Half-brother?
FATHER:	Yes. I have three half-brothers and two half-sisters.
BRICE:	Are you the only whole one in the family?
FATHER:	Oh, keep quiet! And sit still until the plane gets here.
BRICE:	Daddy?
FATHER:	What is it?
BRICE:	Has Uncle Louie got any children?

FATHER:	No.	
BRICE:	Why?	
FATHER:	Because he's never been married before.	
BRICE:	Ohhhh…Daddy?	
FATHER:	What do you want?	
BRICE:	My teacher ain't got any children.	
FATHER:	I can't help it.	
BRICE:	Why?	
FATHER:	Now listen, Snooks. It's almost one o'clock in the morning and I don't feel like answering a lot of nonsensical questions.	
BRICE:	I want some chewing gum.	
FATHER:	You can't have any chewing gum.	
BRICE:	I want some chewing gum!	
FATHER:	What do you want with chewing gum at one o'clock in the morning?	
BRICE:	I'm hungry.	
FATHER:	Eat an apple.	
BRICE:	No—I want a lollipop!	
FATHER:	You just said you wanted chewing gum! Now, which do you want—a lollipop or chewing gum?	
BRICE:	An ice-cream cone!	
FATHER:	Now that's enough, Snooks! I realize it's way past your bedtime and you don't know what you're saying, but just the same, I'm not going to let you drive me crazy.	
BRICE:	Why?	
FATHER:	Because I'm too tired!	
BRICE:	I'm gonna look for the plane.	
FATHER:	Stay here! Don't go out in front of that rail.	
BRICE:	What's out there?	
FATHER:	That's where the plane lands. I don't want you to get hit by a flying propeller.	
BRICE:	Why?	
FATHER:	You may well ask! Stay here!	

BRICE:	I wanna get on the plane.
FATHER:	It isn't here yet!
SOUND:	OFF STAGE WE HEAR THE DRONE OF A PLANE LANDING
BRICE:	Here it comes, Daddy. (STOP PLANE)
FATHER:	(RISES AND LOOKS OFF) That's not ours. That's a mail plane.
BRICE:	How can you tell?
FATHER:	By the insignia on the fuselage. Passenger planes are different from mail planes.
BRICE:	Are they female?
FATHER:	This mail has nothing to do with male or female. I'm talking about letters!
BRICE:	I want some lettuce!
FATHER:	Stop it! Stand here and watch them load the packages on the plane.
BRICE:	Who's that man, Daddy?
FATHER:	He's the pilot. He drives the plane.
BRICE:	Oh. Has he been horseback riding?
FATHER:	Of course not!
BRICE:	Then why is he wearing that pillow strapped on his—
FATHER:	That's a parachute! All commercial pilots wear them.
BRICE:	Why?
FATHER:	In case something happens to his plane while he's flying he can jump out. The parachute helps him land safely.
BRICE:	Does he land sitting down?
FATHER:	No! He lands on his feet!
BRICE:	Then why did he strap the pillow on his—
FATHER:	I told you it's not a pillow! It's a parachute! And it prevents accidents.
BRICE:	Will I have an accident?
FATHER:	Don't worry—you won't have any accidents!
BRICE:	How do you know?
FATHER:	Because planes today are as safe as automobiles. Safer. There are more accidents in cars than there are in planes.

BRICE:	Why?	
FATHER:	Maybe it's because the pilot isn't always hugging the co-pilot!	
BRICE:	Don't the pilot love the co-pilot?	
FATHER:	Yes—he loves him!	
BRICE:	Then why don't he hug him?	
FATHER:	I don't know—I'll ask him!	
BRICE:	I wanna hug a pilot.	
SOUND:	PLANE	
FATHER:	Oh, stop it!	
VOICE:	(FILTER) Flight number seven—leaving gate thirteen in two minutes. Please check your sleeping space before boarding plane.	
FATHER:	(JUMPING UP) That's us, Snooks. Let's go. Grab one of those bags.	
BRICE:	I'm afraid, Daddy.	
FATHER:	Oh please, Snooks! You talked me into taking you along—it's the middle of the night and I can't leave you here. Come on.	
BRICE:	I ain't going!	
FATHER:	Oh, Snooks!	
BRICE:	I'm afraid you'll throw me off the plane.	
FATHER:	Don't give me any ideas! Come on!	
BRICE:	Awight, Daddy.	
FATHER:	(WHISPERS) Now don't make a sound, Snooks.	
BRICE:	(GOOD AND LOUD) Why?	
FATHER:	Shhhh!	
BRICE:	Who's that pretty lady, Daddy?	
FATHER:	She's the stewardess.	
BRICE:	Does she hug the pilot?	
FATHER:	No. She'll take care of us on the trip.	
BRICE:	I wanna hug the pilot.	
FATHER:	Shhh! Sit down here and take your shoes off.	
STEWARDESS:	(QUIETLY) Good evening. Name, please?	
FATHER:	Higgins. This is my child.	

STEWARDESS:	Upper and lower six—that's right. How old are you, little girl?
BRICE:	I'm seven, and my Daddy's thirty-five. Wanna hug him?
FATHER:	Snooks! She's very tired, Miss. I'll have to get her right to bed—stop peeking in those curtains.
BRICE:	Why?
STEWARDESS:	People are sleeping there, dear. Can I help you undress?
BRICE:	No.
FATHER:	Let the lady help you, Snooks.
BRICE:	Is she gonna help you?
STEWARDESS:	Shhh! I'll unlace your shoes.
BRICE:	I wanna get out!
FATHER:	You can't get out! We're going to take off in a second!
STEWARDESS:	That's right, dear. You'd better take off your shoes.
BRICE:	Are you gonna take off, too?
STEWARDESS:	Uh-huh.
BRICE:	You take off first, then I'll take off.
FATHER:	You'd better let me handle her, Miss.
STEWARDESS:	All right, sir. Call me if you need me. (SHE EXITS)
FATHER:	Come on, Snooks. Climb up the little ladder.
BRICE:	Where?
FATHER:	Right up there—in the upper. That's where you'll sleep.
BRICE:	I don't wanna sleep up there.
FATHER:	Do you want to sleep in the lower?
BRICE:	No.
FATHER:	Then where do you want to sleep?
BRICE:	With the pilot.
FATHER:	Please, Snooks, you'll wake up all the passengers in the plane. Climb up there like a good little girl.
BRICE:	I'm afraid to sleep up there alone.
FATHER:	Don't worry—the angels will take care of you.
BRICE:	Where's the angels, Daddy?

FATHER:	The plane is full of them.
MAN:	(HOLLERS) Ahh—shut up with that racket!
BRICE:	Is that one of the angels, Daddy?
FATHER:	See! I told you to keep quiet—you woke up that man! Now, get undressed.
BRICE:	Awight—Daddy?
FATHER:	Shh. Yes?
BRICE:	Tell me a story.
FATHER:	No. Not tonight.
BRICE:	Waaaahhhhh!
FATHER:	Shhh! All right! All right!
MAN:	Hey—why don't you keep that kid quiet?
FATHER:	I'm awfully sorry, sir. It's her first flight and she's a little nervous. She won't disturb you any more.
MAN:	Okay.
BRICE:	Tell me a story!
FATHER:	You heard what the man said.
BRICE:	If you don't tell me a story I'll hold my breath 'til my face turns blue!
FATHER:	All right—I'll tell you a quick story—but no interruptions. Understand?
BRICE:	Understand.
FATHER:	This is the story of Dick Whittington and his cat.
BRICE:	Ohhhhhh—I like it!
FATHER:	Shhh! Once upon a time there was a little boy named Dick. His parents had died and he—
BRICE:	Whose parents?
FATHER:	Dick's parents. They had—
BRICE:	Dick who?
FATHER:	Dick Whittington!
BRICE:	Who's he?
FATHER:	(HOARSE WHISPER) The boy in the story!
BRICE:	Which story?

FATHER:	(YELLS) The story I'm telling you!
BRICE:	Shhhh!
FATHER:	(WHISPERS) Well, don't interrupt! After Dick's parents died he was very poor, so he took his cat and started out for London. He tried to get a job and—
BRICE:	The cat tried?
FATHER:	No—Dick tried!
BRICE:	Dick who?
MAN:	(A VIOLENT SHOUT) DICK WHITTINGTON!
BRICE:	Ohhhhhhhhhh!
MAN:	Now listen, mister. If you don't make that brat go to sleep I'll bust you right in the nose!
FATHER:	Okay, okay! You hear that, Snooks! If that man starts a fight with me I'll have you to thank for it!
BRICE:	You're welcome, Daddy.
FATHER:	Now finish undressing and go to sleep! And not another sound out of you.
BRICE:	Awight. Goodnight, Daddy.
FATHER:	Goodnight.
BRICE:	Daddy?
FATHER:	What is it now?
BRICE:	Take me down.
FATHER:	What for?
BRICE:	Because I have to get down!
FATHER:	You just got up there!
BRICE:	I can't help it! I wanna get down! Quick!
FATHER:	Ahh, nuts. Why didn't you think of it before you got up there?
BRICE:	'Cause I wasn't thirsty then. I bet you thought I had to—
FATHER:	Never mind what I thought! Goodnight!
BRICE:	Goodnight, Daddy.
MUSIC:	(APPLAUSE)

COMMERCIAL: CLOSING—150 WORDS—52 SECONDS

ANNOUNDER: Friends, a few minutes ago we spoke of the richer flavor of Maxwell House Coffee. It's richer when it's hot—and when it's iced, too—and that's something to remember!

What a treat on a sweltering day….a tall, frosty glass of iced Maxwell House Coffee! Because that mellow, full-bodied Maxwell House flavor stands up even when it's iced! Now here's an extra tip…

MAN: (PLAIN AMERICAN ACCENT) Say, this is the most delicious iced coffee I've ever tasted, Mary! It's Maxwell House, isn't it? How is it the ice doesn't dilute the flavor?

WOMAN: Because it is Maxwell House, Jim. Because it's so rich in flavor! And because I always make it a little stronger when I'm going to ice it.

ANNOUNCER: There you are, friends! There's your recipe for one of the summertime's most delicious drinks…cooling, refreshing iced Maxwell House, made just a little stronger. Serve it tomorrow, and let the weather man go hang!

MUSIC: PLAY-OFF

MUSIC: THEME—FADES FOR:

CONTE: Which just about runs us out of our allotment of seconds, but we'll be back again next Thursday at Maxwell House Coffee Time. Fanny Brice as Baby Snooks, Frank Morgan, who appears with us through the courtesy of Metro-Goldwyn-Mayer, Hanley Stafford, and Meredith Willson.

Until next Thursday then, this is John Conte saying goodnight and good luck from the makers of Maxwell House…the coffee that's always…good to the last drop!

MUSIC: (APPLAUSE)

MAXWELL HOUSE PRESENTS "GOOD NEWS OF 1938" MAY 5, 1938 #27

CAST

1. Ted Pearson
2. Robert Young
3. Clark Gable
4. Florence Rice
5. Una Merkel
6. Fanny Brice
7. Frank Morgan
8. Judy Garland
9. Meredith Willson and orchestra
10. Max Terr Chorus

MAXWELL HOUSE MAY 5, 1938 ROUTINE (REVISED)

OPENING

BAND – "OH MAMMA"

WILLSON – YOUNG

GARLAND – "GOD'S COUNTRY"

MORGAN SPOT

COMMERCIAL

BAND – "I BELIEVE IN MIRACLES"

"MANHATTAN MELODRAMA" – GABLE – YOUNG – RICE

STATION BREAK

BABY SNOOKS

GARLAND – "HOW DEEP IS THE OCEAN"

GABLE AND MERKEL

COMMERCIAL

CONCERT HALL – "SCHUBERT'S SERENADE"

MORGAN – YOUNG

CLOSING

PEARSON:	Maxwell House Coffee presents ... Good News of 1938! (MUSIC IN AND FADE)
PEARSON:	Another hour behind the scenes in Hollywood, brought to you by Maxwell House Coffee from Metro-Goldwyn-Mayer, home of the screen's greatest stars. So imagine yourself with us on Metro's Stage Thirty, where tonight you will meet Una Merkel, Florence Rice and your old friends Fanny Brice and Hanley Stafford, Frank Morgan, Judy Garland, Robert Young—tonight's guest of honor, Clark Gable—and Meredith Willson, who starts our program with "Oh, Mamma."

"OH, MAMMA" – ORCHESTRA

(APPLAUSE)

PEARSON:	And here is our host—Robert Young!
YOUNG:	Thank you, Ted—good evening, ladies and gentlemen.
WILLSON:	Hello, Bob.
YOUNG:	Hello, Meredith.
WILLSON:	Say Bob, I want to apologize for the way we treated you on your first program last week. I behaved like a heel.
YOUNG:	That's perfectly natural, Meredith, don't give it a thought.
WILLSON:	Oh, thanks. (HE THINKS A SECOND) What did you say?
YOUNG:	Look, I'm willing to let bygones be bygones. Furthermore, I think that the musical number you just played was very good.
WILLSON:	Well, I'm glad you liked it.
YOUNG:	But I have one suggestion.
WILLSON:	Oh. Er—Frank Morgan said you didn't know very much about music, Bob. Is that a fact?
YOUNG:	That's very true, Meredith. I like to go to concerts, and I enjoy a good dance band, but I certainly wouldn't set myself up as an authority.

WILLSON:	I see. But—you have a suggestion on that last number?
YOUNG:	Just a small thing.
WILLSON:	Is it a suggestion or another insult?
YOUNG:	Why, Meredith, I can't recall insulting you—but if I did, allow me to say it was absolutely intentional. Okay?
WILLSON:	Say, listen Mr. Wisenheimer, you better watch those smart cracks!
YOUNG:	Why, Meredith! I didn't realize you were so bellicose.
WILLSON:	Never mind my physique! I just happen to know that you've been going around telling people I'm a dope.
YOUNG:	Well what of it?
WILLSON:	Just this! Some day you're gonna call somebody a dope that's *not* a dope, and then you'll have your face pushed in. Now say you're sorry!
YOUNG:	Okay. I'm sorry you're a dope.
WILLSON:	That's different. Now tell me — what was the flaw that your musical ear detected in the number we just played?
YOUNG:	Now Meredith, I've already told you that as far as music is concerned, I'm strictly an amateur.
WILLSON:	In other words, you admit you know nothing about music.
YOUNG:	Exactly.
WILLSON:	All right. Then let's hear your criticism.
YOUNG:	Well—I just happened to notice that in the contrapuntal passage that began in the third bar of the last coda, the bassoon player who was supposed to take an F sharp as the top of the subdominant, played it as G flat.
WILLSON:	Maybe I am a dope.
YOUNG:	Now you're talking.
WILLSON:	Not that I admit you're right, understand!
YOUNG:	No?
WILLSON:	Oh no! Why that bassoon player is one of the finest musicians in the country, at any price! You know I hire all my men strictly on merit.
YOUNG:	All right—ask the bassoon player if I'm right.
WILLSON:	I'll take the dare! Oh Cedric!

STOOGE:	Yes?	
WILLSON:	Cedric, this is Mr. Young. Bob—shake hands with Cedric Willson.	
YOUNG:	Er—what's the name?	
WILLSON:	The name is just a coincidence.	
YOUNG:	Mm Hmmmm!—Strictly on merit!	
WILLSON:	Did you hear what Mr. Young said about the number, Cedric?	
STOOGE:	Sure.	
WILLSON:	Well, what were you playing?	
STOOGE:	The Stars and Stripes Forever.	
WILLSON:	Stars and Stripes Forever! We played that two weeks ago!	
STOOGE:	I don't care, it's my favorite number!	
WILLSON:	Cedric, come outside in the alley with me!	
STOOGE:	I don't wanna!	
WILLSON:	Come on!	
STOOGE:	Meredith, you better not touch me, because when we get home, tonight I'll tell ma!	

(THEY AD LIB THEIR WAY OFF THE STAGE)

YOUNG: Strictly on merit he hires his brother. Well, ladies and gentlemen, if the band can pull itself together and all play the same number on merit, Judy Garland will sing, "God's Country." Come on Judy!

"GOD'S COUNTRY" – GARLAND & ORCHESTRA

(APPLAUSE)

MORGAN: Bob! Oh, Bob!
YOUNG: Hello, Frank.
MORGAN: Bob, have you any idea what I've been doing lately?
YOUNG: Must I guess?
MORGAN: This is serious, Bob. I have been making a study of myself.
YOUNG: Loafing again, huh?
MORGAN: Why not? What? No, Bob. I mean it. I have looked at myself from all angles…and I find that I am a very unusual man.
YOUNG: I could have told you that myself, Frank.
MORGAN: (PLEASED) You could?

YOUNG: Certainly, although I don't think "unusual" is quite the word. I think "odd" is a little closer.

MORGAN: Yes, well you're just jealous, Bob, because you KNOW that after all...the WOMAN APPEAL on this program is Frank Morgan.

YOUNG: What's this all about, Frank?

MORGAN: Well, I feel that being a man about town...a raconteur...a bon vivant...a bit of a rake and a gadabout, it's silly for me to give away my company for nothing.

YOUNG: I still gather no sense from what you're talking about.

MORGAN: In short, I'm going to open a Personal Escort Service.

YOUNG: Oh, Morgan, the Gigolo?

MORGAN: Don't be old fashioned, Bob....a Gigolo escorts a lady simply for the money that's in it, but I work on a different principle. My motto is..."*Ladies*...your pleasure is my business...and business is pleasure." WOW!

YOUNG: I think I've got a better slogan for you, Frank. "Morgan's Personal Escort Service...Don't let a dull-dim-witted-dopey escort bore you all evening, ladies...Let Frank Morgan do it!

MORGAN: Yes, well why not? After all, what has Clark Gable got that I won't be able to use in my business?

YOUNG: Don't tell me you've got Clark Gable mixed up in this goofy proposition.

MORGAN: Why Bob...Gable is a natural for this thing. He's one of the few men who has that certain Morgan-savoire-faire. I've made him vice-president and I'll rent out his services as an escort for ten dollars an evening...with tuxedo, $12.50. I'll make money hand over fist. Viva La France!

YOUNG: Morgan, have you consulted Gable about this?

MORGAN: No—but will he be surprised when he wakes up in the morning and sees the ads in the paper!

YOUNG: Yes, and won't you be surprised when you wake up in the hospital! You'd better get somebody else...for your Special Escort Service!

MORGAN: Well, who would you suggest?

YOUNG: How about Meredith Willson?

MORGAN: Willson? Do you think he's good—?

YOUNG: Yes, I think so.

MORGAN: Well, you know the old saying, "Au royaume des aveugles les borgnes sont rois! (GIGGLES) Willson...Hmmmm...that's a laugh...

SOUND: (PHONE BELL RINGS)

YOUNG: I'll get it...Hello...

GIRL: (FILTER MIKE) Hello, is this the Personal Escort Service?

YOUNG: Just a moment. It's for you, Frank.

MORGAN: Oh...my first customer. Hello...MORGAN'S Personal Escort Service...Head Escort speaking.

GIRL: (FILTER MIKE) This is Owendolyn La Forge. I would like to hire Clark Gable as my escort tonight. I'm *so* lonesome!

MORGAN: I'm sorry Mr. Gable isn't available tonight, Gwendolyn. But, I've got a real thrill for you. I think I might be able to GET YOU FRANK MORGAN! How's that?

GIRL: No thanks! I'd rather be lonesome by myself! (HANGS UP)

YOUNG: What did she say, Frank?

MORGAN: How do you like that, she wants Gable. I offer her a barrel of flour and she wants a biscuit. If I didn't know that old saying "The customer's always right," I'd swear that Gwendolyn is nuts!...

(APPLAUSE)

(MUSIC BRIDGE)

(FIRST HALF OF SHOW)

PEARSON: You know...Most men are pretty particular about coffee—know a good cup of coffee when they taste one. Maybe they don't always say so when they don't like the coffee...but they're pretty apt to declare themselves when they do like it. And I guess most wives realize that.

So...I just wonder if something like this hasn't happened to you—after your husband has left for the office in the morning, you've discovered he's left his coffee cup still half full. You wonder about it...because you know he's always been fond of coffee. Now then...maybe that very night you and he met down town for dinner and with the dessert he said...

SOUND: (CUP SET IN SAUCER)

MAN: This coffee's grand, Madge. Think I'll have another cup. (CALLS) Oh, waiter, another cup of coffee, please.

PEARSON: And there you have it. So if by any chance your husband has been a little half-hearted lately in his enjoyment of the coffee you are serving, I think I can help you. Here's my suggestion—try Maxwell House Coffee. There's coffee I'm pretty sure he'll really like…a blend that's so extra smooth so really mellow in flavor…so roaster rich in full bodied goodness. Yes…it's got everything a man looks for in his cup of coffee…everything that'll bring him back for a second cup.

Get a pound of Maxwell House Coffee tomorrow. Serve it at breakfast and dinner. See if you both don't agree that this is delicious coffee—coffee with that friendly stimulation that buoys you up and never lets you down.

(MUSIC BRIDGE)

YOUNG: Meredith Willson's strictly-on-merit orchestra now plays, "I Believe In Miracles."

MORGAN: Yes, and here I am to prove it…Morgan, the Miracle-Man with the ladies.

WILLSON: Wait a minute, Frank. Are you going to start with that Special Escort business again?

MORGAN: Why not, Willson? After all, remember you're talking to Morgan, the great authority on love. Come around sometime and take a few lessons.

WILLSON: You're going to give me lessons? (PROP LAUGH) Me, Willson, the Don Juan of Paris—plus a change plus c'est le meme chose…In plain English, everybody calls me "Cupid."

MORGAN: Oh, I know that.

WILLSON: You know everybody calls me "Cupid?"

MORGAN: Cupid? I thought you said "Stupid!"

WILLSON: Go away, Frank!

"I BELIEVE IN MIRACLES" – ORCHESTRA

(APPLAUSE)

YOUNG: Several years ago Clark made his first long stride toward stardom in MGM's great picture "Manhattan Melodrama." Tonight, with the aid of Florence Rice and myself, Clark turns back the pages of Hollywood history, to re-enact one of his most beloved roles—Blackie Gallagher. I present him now—Clark Gable!

(APPLAUSE)

YOUNG: And now, Ted—a brief synopsis leading up to our scene tonight, if you please.

(MUSIC BRIDGE)

PEARSON: Manhattan Melodrama is the story of two great friends, and a girl...Blackie Gallagher, played by Clark Gable, and Jim Waide, played by Bob Young, grew up together in New York's East Side. As kids, Blackie fought Jim's fights—but when Blackie fell off a burning excursion boat, it was Jim who dove into the river to try and save him.

Jim Wade was a scholarly kid—Blackie Gallagher liked to play. He was always lucky at dice—or tricking his friends as a gag. At the death of their parents, a kindly old man adopted the both of them. Blackie saw his beloved foster father killed in a riot by the hooves of police horses. He swore he'd get even with cops. Jim went to law school—became assistant district attorney. Blackie opened a gambling house. Worlds apart, they remained dear friends.

Let us look into Blackie Gallagher's gambling house now. The Police have just finished a mock raid, as Blackie's girl friend, Eleanor, (FADING) played by Florence Rice, enters his private office.

(DOOR OPENS AND CLOSES)

ELEANOR: (QUIETLY) Hello, Blackie.

BLACKIE: Oh...hi, honey. Oh, wait till you hear this. I got a present for you...a yacht.

ELEANOR: A yacht?

BLACKIE: Yeah. Won it betting odd and even with a feller. Let's go look it over, huh?

ELEANOR: Thanks...you're getting better all the time. Some night you'll win somebody's aunt in a dice game—

BLACKIE: Huh? Say, snap out of it, baby. The man wanted to gamble—and I won. That's all.

ELEANOR: Sure—that's all. That's all it amounts to you, Blackie. Everything in life can be paid off in chips. A yacht—that someone dreamed about, and thought about, and planned.

BLACKIE: —And built—and I won it on a bet.

ELEANOR: I think it's rotten. Rotten through and through.

BLACKIE: What is?

ELEANOR: Everything about this place. The way you won that boat, that ridiculous raid you just had—you knew the police were coming.

BLACKIE: And *they* knew I knew they were coming—and *I* knew they knew—oh, work it out yourself.

ELEANOR: It's a silly, stupid farce—and it's not funny.

BLACKIE: It pays off in dollar bills, baby—and that's what counts. That's what buys those pretty green things you wear on your ears, and those shiny rings you've got, and those—

ELEANOR: Who wants them? I'm not in love with Cartier's—I'm in love with you! Blackie—get out of it! Take me out of it—

BLACKIE: Come here in my arms.

ELEANOR: But Blackie.

BLACKIE: (NICELY) Shut up.

ELEANOR: Please, Blackie—listen.

BLACKIE: Shut up.

ELEANOR: Oh, dearest…Let's—let's go look at the yacht.

BLACKIE: (LAUGHS) Okay.

(MUSIC BRIDGE)

ELEANOR: Oh, it's a grand yacht, Blackie. Let's sit down here.

BLACKIE: Okay.

ELEANOR: Oh…it's so lovely—restful.

BLACKIE: *You're* lovely—and not so restful.

ELEANOR: A night like this—a place like this—they're *real*, Blackie. They're beautiful, they're clean, they—don't they do something to you—inside?

BLACKIE: You bet.

ELEANOR: Darling, listen. Now that you've got this boat—let's go away on it. To the South Seas, the Orient, the Mediterranean—wherever we want to. And we'll have quiet, peaceful days—and nights like this one.

BLACKIE: (KIDDING) That'd be dandy. We could work out hundreds of crossword puzzles, and play double canfield.

ELEANOR: Be serious, Blackie. Take this chance—get away from the cheap hoodlums that hang around you like so many flies—from graft, rackets, gambling houses.

BLACKIE: Now, wait a minute! This is me! And that's what you've got—that's what you fell in love with!

ELEANOR: You're wrong! (SOFTLY) I fell in love with a very little boy who is playing with a great box of matches—and I don't want my little boy to get burned.

BLACKIE: Come here, honey. He's gonna get burned—and he's gonna love it. Kiss me.

ELEANOR: Don't, Blackie.

BLACKIE: Say, what's got into you tonight?

ELEANOR: It's not tonight, it's every night. Worrying about you, wondering about you, hating everything you do, hating everyone you see.

BLACKIE: Now I know you're going to kiss me.

ELEANOR: Oh, Blackie…(SIGHS)

BLACKIE: Oh, say—I got tickets for the Knockout Hogan-Tony Perrino fight next week—how about it?

ELEANOR: Okay, Blackie.

(MUSIC BRIDGE)

(CROWD NOISES)

JIM: (SHOUTS) Blackie.

BLACKIE: Jim! (DELIGHTED) Why, Jim! Say, what are you doing up here with all these low classed people?

JIM: I haven't seen a fight since you and I cleaned up on the O'MALLEY brothers…Remember, Blackie?

BLACKIE: Do I…

JIM: Is Knockout Hogan as good as you?

BLACKIE: Never seen Hogan? I'll have you meet him some time—nice guy. If I'd known you could have come—I'd have made my girl stay home—she's in there, waiting for me. Where are you sitting?

JIM: Section 19…row double J.

BLACKIE: Why, that's practically in Younkers! Here—you take my ticket. Get a good look at Hogan!

JIM: (LAUGHS) No, thanks—but I wish I had your influence! Where are you?

BLACKIE: Don't know—but it better he good.

JIM:	Same old Blackie—row one—seat one at everything.
BLACKIE:	I've got a reputation to live up to—how'd it look if I sat way back in the second row?
SOUND:	ROAR FROM CROWD
BLACKIE:	Perrino must be coming in…Wait 'till you hear what they hand Hogan—the Champ. How're things down on Center Street? I hear you're the guy who really runs the District Attorney's office.
JIM:	I wish I did. I've just been handed the toughest… (LOUDER CHEER)
BLACKIE:	Hogan must have come in.
JIM:	I've been meaning to call you, Blackie. Do you know anything about a West Side hoodlum called "Pants" Riordan?
BLACKIE:	(GRIMLY) I know *everything* about him.
JIM:	I've got an indictment against him…first degree robbery…and I can get a conviction but everybody's putting pressure on me…even the biggest boys in the party…to go light on him. Let him take a plea of third degree.
BLACKIE:	(SHARPLY) You're not gonna do it! You don't play ball with them grafters. You never did, and you're not gonna start now!
JIM:	I know that, too. But if I could only figure out where the pressure was coming from…
SOUND:	TREMENDOUS ROAR FROM CROWD
BLACKIE:	Fight must be on. But don't worry your head about where the pressure comes from—that guy's got 'em fixed right up to the Angel Gabriel. You're getting it from everybody down the line—but you're gonna fight it! Jim Wade is the one guy money don't talk to—and he never will be.
JIM:	Just listen to how you talk. Remember that old saying about practicing and preaching?
BLACKIE:	Listen to me, pal—you're big stuff, see? Me, I'm the flash—I'm the boy with the ready money—but *you're* going places.
JIM:	Yes…but where?
BLACKIE:	I'll tell you where. To a great big house in Washington that's all done up in white paint. You're a cinch, kid. You're on the level, everybody knows it—and that's what pays off in the end. So you're not gonna let them political sharp shooters shove you behind the eight ball! Try it—and I'll personally bust you right in the nose.

JIM:	(GRINNING) You never saw the day you were big enough. Which reminds me—how about watching Mr. Hogan push Mr. Perrine around?
BLACKIE:	Yeah. When are we gonna get together again? It's been weeks.
JIM:	How about tomorrow night?
BLACKIE:	Saturday?....Can't. Biggest night in the week for me. How's Sunday?
JIM:	No...Bar Association.
BLACKIE:	Monday then....
JIM:	I'm starting the Riordan trial Monday. It'll tie me up every day and night for a week.
BLACKIE:	Oh, well, I'll give you a ring.
JIM:	(LAUGHS) That's how we always wind up.
	(TREMENDOUS CHEER)
JIM:	What's the matter?
BLACKIE:	Fight must be over.
JIM:	Over? I wonder who won?
BLACKIE:	Hogan.
JIM:	Ho do *you* know?
BLACKIE:	I bet on him...didn't I?
	(MUSIC BRIDGE)
	(FADES INTO AUTO DRIVING AND UNDISTINGUISHABLE FILTER VOICE)
BLACKIE:	Hey, driver—turn the radio up higher...
STAFFORD:	Okay, boss.
	(VOICE ON FILTER BECOMES DISTINCT)
VOICE:	(FILTER) And for District Attorney—Jim Wade, 180,516; Panker, 102,218...and here's news hot off the press. Panker concedes his defeat to Wade...the new district attorney of New York—Jim Wade.
BLACKIE:	That's enough, driver. Turn it off. Good old Jim. You know, Eleanor—that fellow's bound for the White House. Which reminds me...(AUTO HORN)...I promised to meet Jim at half past twelve. It's after that now...we were going to celebrate his election. Listen, honey—you've got to do me one great big favor.

ELEANOR:	That's out! This is once you don't pick on this little girl. Entertaining your gun men pals is bad enough. But politicians—no, thanks.
BLACKIE:	But you've got to, honey—Jim's my best friend. He'll probably be out in front of the City Hall waiting for me. You've seen him.
ELEANOR:	Yes.
BLACKIE:	Take him to the Cotton Club. I'll meet you there. I've got to meet Eddie Morgan, and give him a chance to get his dough back.
ELEANOR:	Oh—all right, Blackie!

(MUSIC BRIDGE...FADES INTO HARLEM TUNE AS BACKGROUND)

JIM:	And so ends the reading of this week's success story. Send in twenty-five cents for our little booklet...telling how Jim Wade does it in ten easy lessons...
ELEANOR:	That's grand...And...I've finally met Blackie's little white God.
JIM:	(LAUGHS) Should I flap my wings for you?
ELEANOR:	(SOBERLY) No...
JIM:	Dance?
ELEANOR:	No...Let's talk some more.
JIM:	It's three in the morning.. Do you think Blackie will show up?
ELEANOR:	I—I doubt it ... I've waited for him before.
JIM:	Well when you see him, say hello to him for me...tell him, I'm sorry he couldn't make it.
ELEANOR:	All right—and when Blackie talks of you now, I'll know what he means...
JIM:	Maybe I'd better take you home.
ELEANOR:	All right. Let's go, Mr. Wade.
JIM:	Jim.
ELEANOR:	Jim.

(MUSIC BRIDGE)

SOUND:	DOOR OPENS AND CLOSES.

(SHE HUMS A BIT)

SOUND:	LIGHT CLICK

ELEANOR:	Oh…Blackie…Blackie!…Wake up.
BLACKIE:	(WAKING UP) Oh…ah…Hullo. Fell asleep waiting for you…Where's Jim…
ELEANOR:	Did you have a nice time at the Cotton Club?
BLACKIE:	Me?…Oh, I'm sorry about that, honey…I was way ahead and I couldn't quit.
ELEANOR:	*I* had a marvelous time.
BLACKIE:	I knew you would…Do you good to go out with a gentleman like Jim once in a while.
ELEANOR:	Do me good? He spoiled me. He opened doors for me…Blackie…helped me in and out of the car…Imagine…He was like that all night. Stayed right with me…no table hopping…no making dice out of the sugar cubes…Why, he wouldn't even kiss me goodnight. He even thanked me for being with him.
BLACKIE:	Sounds kind of dull.
ELEANOR:	I wish I could get just one dull evening like that out of you once a year.
BLACKIE:	(LAUGHS) You couldn't stand it…Too rich for your blood.
ELEANOR:	Blackie.
BLACKIE:	Huh?
ELEANOR:	Have you ever figured any further ahead than fifteen minutes?
BLACKIE:	Sure…Right now I've got bets on the World's Series next October.
ELEANOR:	I don't mean that…I mean us…You and me…Have you ever imagined where we might end up?
BLACKIE:	…Say, Jim must have had a terrific effect on you tonight.
ELEANOR:	Terrific…I saw so much I haven't got…and want…Security…consideration…a shelter…Blackie, some place to get in out of the rain….I only tasted them tonight. But I got enough to know I want them more than anything else in this world.
BLACKIE:	(KIDDING) Trying to make an honest man out of me?
ELEANOR:	Why not? It's been done…You love me…don't you?
BLACKIE:	Sure….sure I do—but…
ELEANOR:	And I love you…Blackie, let's live like human beings…Let's quit running around like a pack of wolves…Let me have what I want…Marriage…a home…

BLACKIE:	(TURNS ON HER) You're talking a lot of hooey…That little place with roses around the door…babies…stuff like that…you're not the type…you'd go crazy!
ELEANOR:	Blackie, that's not true.
BLACKIE:	Shut up and let me talk. You got a big load of Jim tonight, and outside of these crazy notions, it was probably good for you. But get this…Jim's as much out of your class as he is outa mine…Why, I used to get ideas listening to Jim, too. Ideas about being something…but I forgot them because they're not my stuff. I'm goin' home.
ELEANOR:	Blackie.
BLACKIE:	Yeah…
ELEANOR:	Goodbye, Blackie…
BLACKIE:	What's this?…Now, honey, don't be silly…
ELEANOR:	I'm not silly…I was once, I'm all right now…I know what I'm after…I know where I want to go. You see, Blackie, up to a minute ago I loved you very dearly, and all that really mattered to me was you…But right this minute—I can't even remember having been in love with you. It's goodbye, Blackie.
BLACKIE:	You mean that?
ELEANOR:	Yes.
BLACKIE:	Okay…Goodbye…
	(DOOR OPENS AND CLOSES SOFTLY)
	(MUSIC BRIDGE. MUSIC BECOMES HILARIOUS…FADES FOR:)
ELEANOR:	Oh, Jim…This is the happiest New Year's I ever had.
JIM:	…And Eleanor…what you told me about Blackie…you're sure there's nothing any more?
ELEANOR:	It's all gone, Jim…It's dead, buried and forgotten. Blackie is nothing but a swell guy that I once knew…
JIM:	Well, then…
ELEANOR:	Well then…what?
JIM:	Well then…Happy New Year, Eleanor.
ELEANOR:	Happy New Year, Jim…

	(HILARIOUS MUSIC UP…FADE FOR:)
	(RADIO KEY FLASH A LA WINCHELL)
VOICE:	(FILTER) April 16…Jim Wade, district attorney…Weds Eleanor Jones…
	(KEY FLASH)
VOICE:	(FILTER) June 26, Jim Wade is nominated for Governor of New York State…
	(MUSIC UP AGAIN…AND FADE FOR)
BLACKIE:	Eleanor.
ELEANOR:	Oh—Hello, Blackie.
BLACKIE:	I saw you eatin' alone here—so—well—I thought I'd come over and say hello. What you doin' eatin' alone?
ELEANOR:	Sit down, Blackie.
BLACKIE:	You look worried. Are you—are you happy?
ELEANOR:	You mean, with Jim? Very.
BLACKIE:	Yeah? Then—what's wrong?
ELEANOR:	It's about Jim—and you—and me. Someone is trying to hurt Jim Blackie by—well—by bringing up your friendship with him—
BLACKIE:	Hmmmmm…
ELEANOR:	He says that he has proof that Jim's been shielding you, and—well, you know the rest. Jim insists it won't hurt him in his campaign—but—I've heard different.
BLACKIE:	It ain't true—but a lot of mud throwin' ain't gonna help Jim. Who is this guy?
ELEANOR:	His name is Snow…He has a grudge against Jim—and he's waiting until just before the election to spring everything..
BLACKIE:	Snow. I know him. Sure, sure—I'll look him up—maybe I'll talk to him. You know, Jim's headed for the White House. He's square. Well, give my regards to the big shot, will ya?
	(MUSIC BRIDGE)
NEGRO:	Great game here at Madison Square Garden tonight.
BLACKIE:	Yeah…Go out and get me a pack of cigarettes, will you, porter? Here—you can keep the change…

NEGRO:	Oh...yas suh...
	(PAUSE)
SNOW:	(COMING IN) Hello, Gallagher. What's on your mind? It had better be important—getting me in here in this room in the middle of a game.
BLACKIE:	There never was anything more important to you, Snow, than being here right now.
SNOW:	What is this? Say—isn't there anybody in here but us?
BLACKIE:	(QUIETLY) Only us.
SNOW:	Gallagher. What are you going to do?
BLACKIE:	Just a little favor for a friend!
	(THREE SHOTS...MUSIC TAKING AWAY THE THIRD ONE...AND FADE FOR:)
BLACKIE:	Eleanor, you're crazy—comin' here to the jail like this. Suppose somebody spotted you. I can just see the headlines—"D. A.'s wife in secret visit to slayer."...That'd look fine...
ELEANOR:	Blackie—I had to come. I've got to know—did you do it?
BLACKIE:	What do you think?
ELEANOR:	I don't know what to think.
BLACKIE:	You've known me a long time. Ever know me to bump off a guy?
ELEANOR:	No, but—this is different.
BLACKIE:	Do you love Jim?
ELEANOR:	More than anything in the whole world. Blackie, I never knew what love was, until I met Jim. You see—
BLACKIE:	Then if you love Jim so much—and want to see him Governor—keep quiet. (QUIET) You don't know that guy like I know him. Above everything else in the world, Jim is District Attorney! Remember that. You tell him about that day we met in the restaurant and he'll have you on the stand...Then where is he?
ELEANOR:	But you—this means your life—
BLACKIE:	What's my life...Listen—you keep your mouth shut.
ELEANOR:	You know, Blackie—for a while I was almost ashamed that I ever loved you...I'm not now—I'm proud.
BLACKIE:	That's fine—I think you're okay too.

GUARD:	Time's up.
BLACKIE:	Yeah—so long, Eleanor.
ELEANOR:	(WHISPERS) Goodbye—Blackie.

(MUSIC UP AND FADE FOR:)

JIM:	(WITH EFFORT) Gentlemen of the Jury, in finding Blackie Gallagher guilty of murder, we are faced with more than the avenging of one death. We are faced with a choice which we must make. Either we can surrender to an epidemic of crime and violence which will destroy our homes and community—or we can serve warning to the host of other criminals and gangsters that they're through. Many years ago—when an excursion boat burned—I made a boyish attempt to save Blackie Gallagher's life…Today—I demand his death!
JURY FOREMAN:	We—the Jury—find Blackie Gallagher guilty of murder—in the first degree.

(A MUSIC FLARE OFF)

JIM:	I'm sorry, Blackie—I had to do it.
BLACKIE:	Okay, kid…I can take it…And can you give it out!…So long.

(MUSIC BIG)

(APPLAUSE)

END

(STATION BREAK)

YOUNG:	Thank you, Clark Gable, for that swell job as Blackie Gallagher. And say…
GABLE:	Yeah?
YOUNG:	How about a steaming cup of Maxwell House Coffee right now?
GABLE:	Sounds great to me. I'm sold on Maxwell House Coffee, you know.
YOUNG:	Good, so am I. After a hard shooting schedule and dinner time comes around—a cup of Maxwell House Coffee certainly does give you a lift.
GABLE:	Well, the real test of coffee, as far as I'm concerned, Bob, is around a campfire when you're fishing or hunting. And, believe me, Maxwell House goes along with me on my trips.

PEARSON: Thanks Clark, and friends, it's time right now for that friendly custom, a steaming fragrant cup of Maxwell House—the coffee most men like. So we're inviting all of you—everyone here and those of you listening to Good News in your homes, to join us in a cup of this coffee that's good to the last drop. And Meredith—how about some of that good music that goes with it?

MUSIC: FULL & FADE FOR:

PEARSON: We pause briefly for station identification.

MUSIC: UP & FADE

(AFTER STATION BREAK)

YOUNG: This is Bob Young again and we continue our Good News of 1938 with some of the highlights in our show still to come, more of Clark Gable…Baby Snooks…Judy Garland and the Concert Hall.

BABY SNOOKS

YOUNG: Into each life a little rain must fall, but when Snooks was born it really poured! Tonight we find Baby Snooks and her daddy, played by Hanley Stafford, seated at a table in a railroad station restaurant grabbing a pre-train snack…Enter now that terrible tantalizing tot—BABY SNOOKS!

(APPLAUSE…PLAY ON)

FATHER: Take off your coat, Snooks, and I'll hang it up right here next to Daddy's.

BRICE: Awight.

FATHER: There…Now, let's eat in a hurry.

BRICE: What's that sign on the wall, daddy?

FATHER: It's an old fashioned sign they used to hang in restaurants. It says "Watch your hat and coat."

BRICE: I'll watch 'em, daddy.

FATHER: Never mind that. Just sit down—and no stalling with your food—we only have five minutes to catch the train.

BRICE: Where we going, daddy?

FATHER: I've told you a dozen times. We're going to visit Grandma.

BRICE: Ohhh…Why are all these people eating here?

FATHER: They have to catch a train, too.

BRICE:	The same train we have to catch?	
FATHER:	Yes—I guess so.	
BRICE:	It's gonna be awful crowded at Grandma's ain't it?	
FATHER:	They're not going to Grandma's…Give me that menu—I'll order a quick bite.	
BRICE:	From who?	
FATHER:	From the waitress.	
BRICE:	If she bites me I'll bite her back!	
FATHER:	I'm talking about food!…Sit still…(CALLS)…Oh miss!	
WAITRESS:	Yes, sir?	
FATHER:	I'll have a chicken sandwich and a glass of beer. Bring the little girl a lettuce and tomato salad and some milk.	
WAITRESS:	Yes, sir—right away.	
BRICE:	I don't want no milk, daddy.	
FATHER:	You have to drink milk, Snooks. It'll make you big and strong.	
BRICE:	What are you gonna drink?	
FATHER:	A glass of beer.	
BRICE:	That's what I want!	
FATHER:	Don't be silly—you can't have beer.	
BRICE:	Why?	
FATHER:	Because it'll make you dizzy! Stop squirming in your seat.	
BRICE:	I'm looking to see if the coats are still there, daddy.	
FATHER:	Don't be foolish. Tuck that napkin in your neck—here comes the food.	
WAITRESS:	Here you are, sir…	
	(CLATTER OF DISHES)	
FATHER:	Thanks…Go ahead and eat your salad, Snooks.	
BRICE:	I want some bananas.	
FATHER:	They haven't got any bananas.	
BRICE:	Yes they have! Right there—hanging on a stick!	
FATHER:	You can't have those bananas—they're still green.	

BRICE:	I like 'em!
FATHER:	I know it but they're not ripe!
BRICE:	Why?
FATHER:	Because they're green!
BRICE:	Then I want some beer!
FATHER:	No! It'll make you dizzy! Eat your lettuce!
BRICE:	I don't wanna! The lettuce is no good.
FATHER:	Why not?
BRICE:	'Cause it's green.
FATHER:	What of it?
BRICE:	Well, if it's green it ain't ripe!
FATHER:	Oh, stop that nonsense! Of course it's ripe.
BRICE:	You said the bananas ain't ripe when they're green.
FATHER:	I know I did.
BRICE:	Then why is the lettuce ripe when it's green?
FATHER:	Because that's the color of lettuce when it's ripe!
BRICE:	Well, what color is it when it ain't ripe?
FATHER:	(SHOUTS) GREEN! It's green when it's ripe and it's green when it's not ripe!
BRICE:	Did you drink some beer, daddy?
FATHER:	YES!
BRICE:	Did it make you dizzy?
FATHER:	NO! Hurry up and eat your salad or we'll miss the train!
BRICE:	Awight…Daddy?
FATHER:	What?
BRICE:	I'll just eat the tomatoes—I don't want the lettuce.
FATHER:	(CONTROLLED) Snooks, don't make me yell at you in front of all these people. You simply must eat the lettuce.
BRICE:	Why?
FATHER:	Because it's full of vitamins!
BRICE:	What's vitamins?

FATHER: It's something in your food that gives it the necessary nutriment value. That plate of lettuce has millions of vitamins.

BRICE: I don't see any.

FATHER: I know you don't—but they're in there just the same! You can't see them, you can't taste them, you can't feel them and you can't smell them—but if they weren't there you wouldn't be here!

BRICE: Are you sure you ain't dizzy, daddy?

FATHER: (YELLS) YES, I'M SURE! EAT THAT LETTUCE BEFORE I STUFF IT DOWN YOUR THROAT!

BRICE: Wahhhhhh!

FATHER: What's the matter?

BRICE: I'm afraid of the vitamins!

FATHER: Listen, Snooks—all food has vitamins. And each vitamin has a name.

BRICE: Can I call this one Charlie?

FATHER: No—they're called A B C D E and G.

BRICE: Where's F?

FATHER: There is no F vitamin—just A B C D E and G. And you must eat at least two of them every day.

BRICE: I don't need any today, daddy—I had 'em all yesterday.

FATHER: Where?

BRICE: Mummy gave me alphabet soup.

FATHER: I don't want any excuses, Snooks—we haven't got much time left!...Where's that clock?

BRICE: Right behind you, daddy.

FATHER: Oh...Good heavens—there's only two minutes left and—Snooks! What happened to your lettuce?

BRICE: Huh?

FATHER: You didn't have time to eat it—I just turned my head for a second. Did you hide it?

BRICE: No.

FATHER: Then where is it?

BRICE: The vitamins ate it!

FATHER:	Oh, what's the use. Drink your milk and let's get out of here.
BRICE:	Awight.
FATHER:	Wait—don't gulp it so fast! Snooks—you'll get sick! SNOOKS!
BRICE:	I finished it, daddy…HIC!
FATHER:	You see—now you have the hiccups.
BRICE:	Why?…HIC!
FATHER:	Because you drank the milk so fast!
BRICE:	HIC!…(LAUGHS)…HIC!
FATHER:	Stop laughing!
BRICE:	I can't. My stomach tickles me…HIC!
FATHER:	Here—take a little sugar. That'll make the hiccups go away.
BRICE:	Awight…HIC!
FATHER;	Swallow it. Now drink a little water and hold your breath while I count five…Here…one, two, three, four—
BRICE:	HIC!…(LAUGHS)
FATHER:	I told you to hold your breath while I counted five!
BRICE:	Waaaahhhh!…HIC!
FATHER:	What's the matter?
BRICE:	I held my breath but the hiccup pushed it out…HIC!
FATHER:	Well, drink some more water and hold your breath…Here…One, two, three, four, five…There—now let your breath out.
BRICE:	(BLOWS)
FATHER:	(YELLS) Don't let the water out, too! You blew it all over me!
BRICE:	I'm sorry, daddy.
FATHER:	Oh, well. Are the hiccups gone?
BRICE:	Uh-huh.
FATHER:	Are you sure?
BRICE:	Uh-huh…It's better now…HIC!…(LAUGHS)…It came back again, daddy…HIC!
FATHER:	Oh, my heavens!…(SUDDENLY SHOUTS)…SNOOKS!
BRICE:	Huh?

FATHER:	BOO!...BOO!
BRICE:	(LAUGHS)...HIC! What you doing, daddy?
FATHER:	I'm trying to scare you...BOO!
BRICE:	(LAUGHS)...HIC!
FATHER:	GRRRR! AHHHH! (MAKES WEIRD NOISES) Awwwwkkk!
WAITRESS:	Er—excuse me, sir—is something wrong?
BRICE:	I think my daddy had too much beer!
FATHER:	Nothing of the kind! Er—never mind, miss—everything's all right.
WAITRESS:	Yes, sir.
FATHER:	What's the matter with you, Snooks? You know very well I was only I trying to cure—HIC!
BRICE:	(LAUGHS) Now *you* got 'em, daddy!
FATHER:	(SHOUTS) It's all your—HIC! Give me that sugar. Snooks—do you hear me? HIC! What are you twisting around for?
BRICE:	It's the only way I can watch my coat.
FATHER:	Well, stop it! HIC! You don't see me watching my coat!
BRICE:	You don't have to—some man took yours five minutes ago!
	(APPLUASE)
	(SNOOKS PLAY—OFF)
YOUNG:	Whenever we think of great poetry, our minds inevitable turn to men like Keats, Browning or Shelley, and not to music. We seem to forget that some of our lyric writers are really fine poets. One such famous poet is Irving Berlin. Judy Garland now brings us one of Mr. Berlin's loveliest poems, set to one of his most glorious melodies. "HOW DEEP IS THE OCEAN"
	"HOW DEEP IS THE OCEAN" – GARLAND & ORCHESTRA
	(APPLAUSE)
	MERKEL – GABLE – YOUNG
MERKEL:	Oh, Bob. Hey, Bob!
YOUNG:	Why Una Merkel! I'm glad to see you.
MERKEL:	Well I'm glad to be here, Bob. I always have such a lovely time with you, you're always so considerate and thoughtful, and I've always liked

	you and kinda looked up to you, and I'm always thinking about you, and then of course, I heard Clark Gable was going to be here, too.
YOUNG:	But you're always thinking of *me*.
MERKEL:	I surely am, Clark—I mean Bob. Where IS Clark?
YOUNG:	Wait a minute, Una. Have you got another one of those articles up your sleeve?
MERKEL:	Yes I have, Bob, and I know you'll be crazy about this one, cause I made it up all by myself, from an idea you gave me. You remember you said you'd like to write an article "What I Think of Una Merkel?"
YOUNG:	Yes.
MERKEL:	Well I thought it was a wonderful idea, but I decided I'd rather have Clark Gable write it, so I wrote it.
YOUNG:	You decided you'd rather have Clark write it?
MERKEL:	Yes.
YOUNG:	And then you wrote it.
MERKEL:	Yes.
YOUNG:	Mm-hmmmm. I suppose you'll sell it to Collier's Weekly, and it'll be printed in the New Yorker.
MERKEL:	No, we'll have it printed right here in Los Angeles. I love it out here, don't you, Bob? You meet such nice people. Where's Clark?
YOUNG:	Now listen, Una, one of the jobs I'm supposed to do on this program is to keep the stars from being bothered by interviewers like you. I'm sorry, but you can't talk to Clark Gable now.
MERKEL:	Oh dear!! Well, Bob, in that case, I'll just have to let them print the article the way I've written it.
YOUNG:	Wait a minute! Hey Clark!
GABLE:	(OFF—CALLS TO YOUNG) What is it, Bob?
YOUNG:	You better come over here and defend yourself, I'm leaving right now before the sparks begin to fly.
CLARK:	Well what is it? Oh, hello Una!
MERKEL:	Hello Clark, darling! I heard you just now when you were acting in that perfectly lovely sketch, Manhattan Cocktail, and I thought it was simply grand!
GABLE:	"Manhattan Cocktail"—it's "Melodrama!"

MERKEL: What if it is? Some people like comedy, and some like melodrama.

GABLE: Una, all I'm trying to tell you is, it's not "Manhattan Cocktail", it's "Manhattan Melodrama".

MERKEL: It doesn't make any difference, I never drink anyway. What I really wanted to talk to you about was this article that I've written. It's a wonderful idea, and I'd just like to get your approval on it.

GABLE: Sure! What is it?

MERKEL: It's an article called, "What I think of Una Merkel—By Clark Gable."

GABLE: It sounds interesting—if true.

MERKEL: Well, it's interesting. Do you want to hear it before I send it to the publishers, Clark darling?

GABLE: I think I'd better.

MERKEL: All right, here goes. Quote. "Here's the real lowdown on what I think of Una Merkel. Una was born in one of the most aristocratic counties of the old South, the old South that Margaret Mitchell wrote about and to use a familiar phrase, Una was born with a silver spoon in her mouth."

GABLE: And a mint julep in her hand.

MERKEL: Oh no, it was Daddy had the mint julep in his hand! He went thru a terrible strain before I was born.

GABLE: I imagine he's been thru something *since*, too!

MERKEL: He sure has! Do you know what the doctor said when I was born?

GABLE: Why bring that up?

MERKEL: Well, Clark—how did you know?

GABLE: Look, Una—do me a favor and read me the article on "What I think about Una Merkel," before I write one myself.

MERKEL: Surely, Clark…Let me see—oh, yes…Quote…"Una's childhood was the childhood of any high-spirited Southern girl of gentle breeding—very much like that of the famed heroine Scarlett O'Hara. She was naturally inclined towards acting at a very early age. Her Southern background enabled her to—"

GABLE: What's all this Southern stuff, Una? What's that got to do with what I think of Una Merkel?

MERKEL: Nothing—but I thought it might help get me a part in "Gone With The Wind!"

GABLE:	I see. Well, it's too bad you weren't born in France.
MERKEL:	Why?
GABLE:	Well, we could give Marie Antoinette a plug! Go ahead with the article.
MERKEL:	I guess I'd better start down here at the second paragraph. This first part is all about my size and age and weight and where Mr. Selznick can reach me if he still hasn't found a Scarlett O'Hara—you know.
GABLE:	Oh, sure. Maybe you could throw in a little advertisement to sell your car, too.
MERKEL:	I did.
GABLE:	Go ahead, Una.
MERKEL:	All right. Quote. "Whenever anybody asks me who is my ideal girl—I immediately say, "Una Merkel" quicker than you can say Jack Jobinson." Is that okay with you, Clark?
GABLE:	I'll take Jack Robinson—but don't mind me…Keep punching, Una.
MERKEL:	Quote. "My friends have heard me say, time and again, that Una Merkel is without a doubt the most brilliant, charming, and beautiful young creature that ever walked the earth".
GABLE:	Hold it, Una—isn't that a little immodest?
MERKEL:	Well, Clark, it would be if I were saying it—but don't forget you're the one who's writing this article, and besides it's not really what you'd call drawing the long bow, if you know what I mean. After all, this article should contain facts!
GABLE:	That stops me. Read on, Una.
MERKEL:	All right—it goes on to say…Quote…"I have tried many times to date Una up for an evening, but she is so popular I simply can't get to first base. Of course she has a private telephone number which she only gives to people she thinks an awful lot of—and that number is—" are you listening, Clark?
GABLE:	I'm listening.
MERKEL:	"Una Merkel's private number is Brayant 97800 and you can call me any time after eight, Clark." Interesting article, isn't it?
GABLE:	I don't want any part of it, honey.
MERKEL:	You mean you don't like it so far?
GABLE:	I mean I don't like it! That's not what I think of Una Merkel at all.
MERKEL:	Well, what do you think of Una Merkel?

GABLE:	You want to know?
MERKEL:	Yes.
GABLE:	Ahem...(TO AUDIENCE)...Shall I tell her?
MERKEL:	Yes—tell me. What do you think of Una Merkel?
GABLE:	Lean over, Una—I'll have to whisper.

(BUZZ ... BUZZ... BUZZ)

MERKEL:	Why Clark! And give up writing?
GABLE:	Positively. And I think you can get a job as a cook in Mother Willson's tea-room! So long, Una!

(APPLAUSE)

(PLAY-OFF)

(SECOND HALF OF SHOW)

PEARSON:	Thanks, Bob. (PAUSE) You know...the other day I rode home in the bus behind two housewives who were discussing their favorite topic—their husbands. Said one woman...
1st WOMAN:	One thing I can't seem to do is make coffee that John likes. And yet I've tried brand after brand...
2nd WOMAN:	Well you know, Helen, most men are terribly particular when it comes to coffee. I had the same trouble as you—until I hit on Maxwell House...
PEARSON:	And friends, Maxwell House *does* make a marvelous cup of coffee. So if you've had trouble pleasing your husband with the coffee you serve, why don't you try Maxwell House. It's one coffee most *men* like. They like its rich mellow flavor. They like its full-bodied goodness. They like that feeling it brings of deep-down satisfaction.
	And that's because Maxwell House Coffee is a superb blend of coffees to begin with. Then, it is packed in the super vacuum can so it *reaches* you with all its flavor and goodness sealed in—roaster fresh whenever and wherever you buy it. And we offer you Maxwell House in a choice of two grinds—the special drip grind for all drip...and glass...coffee makers...the regular grind for percolator or boiled coffee. Because we know how important it is to use the right grind for the way you make your coffee.
	And then...we offer Maxwell House in one and two pound cans. If you use lots of coffee, you'll find it thrifty to buy the two-pound size.
	So—choose Maxwell House tomorrow. See if you both don't get more real pleasure from this coffee that's truly...good to the last drop.

	MUSIC BRIDGE
YOUNG:	And now, Meredith Willson opens the doors of our Concert Hall and invites you to listen to another in his series of the World's most beloved melodies. In the past few weeks, you've heard among others, the world's most beloved piano selection, violin solo, and lullaby. Tonight, Meredith plays the world's most beloved Serenade—the Serenade written by the immortal Franz Schubert.
	"SCHUBERT'S SERENADE" – ORCHESTRA
	(APPLAUSE)
SOUND:	(PHONE BELL)
YOUNG:	Hello.
WOMAN:	(FILTER MIKE) Is this Mr. Frank Morgan of the Personal Escort Service?
YOUNG:	No, just a minute—Hey, Morgan, it's again with that personal Escort business.
MORGAN:	Oh, I suppose she wants Gable, too. I'm sick and tired of it. (KEEPS GETTING MORE EXCITED) Here I work my fingers to the bone building up a business and all they wanna do is talk turkey…Gable—Gable—Gable—I've had enough of it. The whole thing is positively insulting—Give me that phone. (YELLS) Hello.
WOMAN:	Hello.
MORGAN:	You and Gable can go jump in the lake!
WOMAN:	What's that? I don't want Gable, I want Frank Morgan.
MORGAN:	Yes, I'll—What? Say, Bob what kind of a woman is this? Hello, this is Frank Morgan, Head Escort.
WOMAN:	Well, Mr. Morgan, I'd like you to call for me at 8:30 sharp. Wear your evening clothes as we will dine at the Trocadero…See the best show and make the rounds of the clubs afterwards.
MORGAN:	Well, that's wonderful. You understand you pay all the checks of course.
WOMAN:	Oh yeah? Well I'll pay nothing. This is your wife and it's about time you took me out, you cheapskate! Now get spiffy right away or I'll send someone after you! Goodbye! (HANGS UP)
MORGAN:	So long follows…see you later! I gotta go home and rehearse—everything happens to me—
	(APPLAUSE)

YOUNG:	It's "Good News" again next Thursday at the same time—when the makers of Maxwell House Coffee bring you another star-studded program…featuring Robert Montgomery—Maureen O'Sullivan—Mickey Rooney—Dennis O'Keefe—Hanley Stafford—Douglas McPhail—Frank Morgan—Fanny Brice, and Meredith Willson and his music. Fanny will sing one of the songs that made her famous on Broadway.
PEARSON:	And I hope you will enjoy Bob Montgomery—Frank Morgan—Meredith Willson—and Robert Young in "If Men Went Marketing as Women Do."
YOUNG:	Remember, your ticket of admission is just your loyalty to Maxwell House Coffee, so be sure to listen in. In the meantime, go to the movies and take the family with you. This is Bob Young saying "Goodnight"—see you next Thursday!
	(APPLAUSE)
	(MUSIC UP)
PEARSON:	(MUSIC CREDITS)
	This is Ted Pearson saying goodnight and good luck for the Makers of Maxwell House—the coffee that is always good to the last drop.

MAXWELL HOUSE COFFEE TIME
JUNE 26, 1941

1. SNOOKS AND DADDY
2. THEME AND CAST INTRODUCTION – "TWO HEARTS THAT PASS IN THE NIGHT"
3. FRANK MORGAN SPOT
4. COMMERCIAL
5. "VALSE"
6. BABY SNOOKS SPOT
7. COMMERCIAL
8. "THE RELUCTANT DRAGON"
9. SIGN-OFF
10. HITCH-HIKE

DIRECTION: (ON CUE)
BRICE: Waaaahhhh!
FATHER: Snooks! What are you crying about?
BRICE: Mummy was nailing a calendar on the wall —
FATHER: Well?
BRICE: She hit her thumb with the hammer!
FATHER: That's nothing to cry about. You should laugh.
BRICE: I did. That's why I'm crying.
FATHER: Well, forget about it.
BRICE: Why do we need a calendar, Daddy?
FATHER: Because it tells us what day it is.
BRICE: Don't you know what day it is?
FATHER: Certainly, it's Thursday.
BRICE: Who told you?

FATHER: The calendar told me.

BRICE: Why?

FATHER: That's how we keep track of the days and months. If we didn't have a calendar how would you know it was Thursday?

BRICE: 'Cause it's the cook's day off.

FATHER: I know that! But if you didn't have a calendar how could you tell when Friday came?

BRICE: It's easy.

FATHER: How?

BRICE: The cook comes back.

FATHER: Forget the cook! The calendar is a very important invention. It's a method of distributing time into certain periods adapted to the purpose of civil life—it spaces off the months and seasons.

BRICE: What's that, Daddy?

FATHER: You know what the seasons are! There are four of them.

BRICE: Yeah?

FATHER: Yes. Let me hear you name the four seasons.

BRICE: Salt, pepper, mustard, and vin—

FATHER: No! There's summertime, wintertime, springtime—and—?

BRICE: And what?

FATHER: What's the other time?

BRICE: Oh, I know!

FATHER: What?

BRICE: It's Maxwell House Coffee Time!

MUSIC: THEME

ANNOUNCER: Yes, ladies and gentlemen, it is Maxwell House Coffee Time—and time to enjoy another pleasant half hour with Frank Morgan, Hanley Stafford, Meredith Willson and his orchestra, and Fanny Brice's inimitable character creation, the one and only Baby Snooks!

BRICE: I didn't do nothing. (APPLAUSE)

ANNOUNCER: And here is our master of ceremonies—your host for the evening—John Conte!

MUSIC:	CONTE AND ORCHESTRA – TWO HEARTS THAT PASS IN THE NIGHT (APPLAUSE)
CONTE:	Thank you, ladies and gentlemen, and good evening. Say, Meredith!
MEREDITH:	Yes, Johnny boy?
CONTE:	I read an item in last night's paper that you had a fire at your house. Is that right?
MEREDITH:	Well, you'd hardly call it a fire. No real damage done—didn't even have to call the fire engines.
CONTE:	Well, what happened?
MEREDITH:	Oh, nothing. I fell asleep in the living room with a lit cigarette in my hand. It fell on the floor and burned up a bear rug.
CONTE:	Is that all?
MEREDITH:	Well, I did get a little excited and knocked over an expensive vase—and Peggy heard the noise and tripped down a flight of stairs. She'll be laid up with a sprained ankle for a couple of weeks, but there was no real damage to speak of.
CONTE:	No.
MEREDITH:	I guess that bear rug'll be hard to replace, though. It's a kind of an heirloom.
CONTE:	Been in the family a long time, eh?
MEREDITH:	No, I bought it in a hockshop for three dollars. But the pawnbroker told me he shot it himself. It was a she bear.
CONTE:	This is getting a little too mixed up for me, Meredith. Why did you say it was an heirloom?
MEREDITH:	Well, it sounds better than saying you bought it in a hockshop for three dollars. But you should hear the story of how this fellow shot that—
CONTE:	I'd love to hear, but not right now. We've got to—
MEREDITH:	John, I guess there's nothing tougher in the world than a female bear. Guy told me this female was seven feet tall, perfectly built, and when she hugged you she could crack all of your ribs!
MORGAN:	(COMING ON) Sounds wonderful! Can she get a friend for me—only not so affectionate!
CONTE:	Frank! (APPLAUSE)
MORGAN:	Who is this lady Tarzan, Meredith? I think I could get in shape for the dame if you—

MEREDITH: Frank! It's a female bear!

MORGAN: You mean she doesn't wear—oh! Bear! Have you been spending your time at the zoo?

MEREDITH: (LAUGHS) You know, after it was over, Peggy and I had a good laugh.

MORGAN: Hmmmm.

MEREDITH: (STILL AMUSED) Yes, sir. When the rug burned I thought of that little joke about the moth who ate a hole in the carpet at the night club.

MORGAN: (YAWNS) Ho hum.

MEREDITH: Peggy really got a boot out of that, yes sir!

MORGAN: Hmmm.

CONTE: All right, Meredith—why did the moth eat a hole in the carpet at the night club?

MEREDITH: He wanted to see the floor show. (LAUGHS) We sure laughed. (THEY FREEZE HIM AND HE FADES OFF) I thought it was pretty funny. Heard it on a radio program…just kind of a pun, that's all. I'm sorry, Frank.

MORGAN: Meredith, those punny jokes of yours get worse every week, but that one sounded like the week after next.

MEREDITH: I guess so. But I just wanted to make Peggy laugh to take her mind off the fire.

MORGAN: My dear boy, a fire's no laughing matter. Even the most trivial conflagration can have tragic results. A tiny spark can cause untold destruction. One forgotten ember might turn a verdant countryside into a desolate waste! Please walk, do not run, to the nearest exit! (Is this Fire Prevention Week?)

CONTE: No, Frank. But it sounds wonderful to hear you so serious.

MORGAN: Thank you, Jockey. You can be quite a delightful fellow when you abandon that external coarseness which I'm sure runs considerably more than skin deep.

CONTE: Wait till I figure that out.

MORGAN: Don't bother. I just want to impress upon your minds the seriousness of fire. Of course, in my house such a thing could never happen.

MEREDITH: Is it all fireproof, Frank?

MORGAN: No, but I happen to own the world's greatest fire dog. Champion Prince von Staugwitz von Gliesen Mutlich auf der Heide Lipschutz the Third.

CONTE: What breed is he?

MORGAN: A mutt. But he cost me three thousand dollars, and looking into his ancestry I found he was part poodle and part bull.

MEREDITH: Which part is bull?

MORGAN: The part about the three thousand doll—no! He was bull on his mother's side, and he displayed all the courage, devotion and intelligence of the breed. After he won the Carnegie medal, he was retired on a government pension, and I was—

CONTE: Wait a minute, Frank. How did the dog win the Carnegie medal?

MORGAN: By a demonstration of the most astute reasoning ever manifested by a member of the animal world. I won't go into all the terrible details, but it was during a fire at my country home that the incident occurred.

MEREDITH: Gee, this is interesting.

MORGAN: I'm beginning to have my doubts. At any rate, when the fire got out of control, and the building appeared doomed, this amazing dog made five trips into the blazing inferno, each time returning with some valuable object that he knew I prized. He laid the bottles at my feet, and just as the side walls were tottering, he dashed into the house once more. The dog soon returned, and when I saw what he was carrying between his teeth I could scarcely believe my eyes.

CONTE: What was he carrying, Frank?

MORGAN: My insurance policy, wrapped in a damp towel. (No wonder the people are starting to call me Munchausen!)

MEREDITH: Well, there are none so blind as those who will not see! Go on, Frank!

MORGAN: Yes. As a matter of fact, the story is not so incredible as it sounds, since my dog received his training fires while he was the mascot of the Chicago Fire Department.

CONTE: How did you get him?

MORGAN: Well, it was only natural that when I resigned as Fire Chief that I should take the dog and—

CONTE: Fire Chief! Are you going to hoodwink the people into believing that you were a fireman, Mr. Morgan?

MORGAN:	Smokey Morgan, sir! For generations the Morgans have been firefighters, and I'm the last of a long line of false alarms! I mean, third alarms!
CONTE:	Well, I know we'd get into that sooner or later.
MORGAN:	So did I—and I hope it isn't too late. (GIGGLES) My grandfather, Hosepipe Morgan, was the first man to invent a fire extinguisher that was absolutely foolproof. Working on the theory that it takes fire to combat fire, my gaffer devised an instrument that shot a stream of gasoline into any small blaze, localizing the intensity and curbing the spread of the flames.
MEREDITH:	Was it good?
MORGAN:	Good? You couldn't hold a candle to it! When he had it finished, he demonstrated before a jeering crowd of skeptics. He began by touching a match to a pile of straw in the middle of City Hall, then aimed his gasoline extinguisher right at the fire! There was a terrific explosion, and when the smoke cleared, the amazement on the faces of the lookers-on was impossible to describe!
CONTE:	The fire was gone!
MORGAN:	Yes—and so was the City Hall! After my grandfather was released from the asylum, I determined to keep up the family tradition by joining the Fire Brigade.
MEREDITH:	This is the part I love! Go on, Frank!
MORGAN:	Meredith, I'm beginning to suspect you of goading me into these things, just so you can say, "Go on, Frank!"
MEREDITH:	Not me! Go on, Frank!
MORGAN:	Yes. Well, I started as a rookie fireman with the Chicago Fire Department, Station Four, Hook and Ladder Nine, and in order to become inured to the bite of the flames, I was forced to take the phlogiston test.
CONTE:	Phlogiston test? What's that?
MORGAN:	A light singe.
CONTE:	I'll have a baldy.
MORGAN:	Trim the sides?
CONTE:	Just on top.
MORGAN:	That'll be forty cen—what are we talking about!
MEREDITH:	Cut it out, John! Tell us about the firehouse, Frank!

MORGAN: Well, my duties were quite dull at first, since I was not allowed to attend fires. But I took great pride in keeping my living quarters spic and span, and I became particularly adept at making up my own bunk. (Well, it's gonna be different next season!)

CONTE: It serves you right! If you'd tell the truth once in a while you wouldn't be so self-conscious about those double-entendre words!

MORGAN: Truth! The Morgans have always lived sans peur at sans raproche! From earliest infancy I was taught the virtue of honesty, and from manhood on I employed only the truth!

CONTE: You employed it!

MORGAN: Well, it's not my fault if there's been a lot of unemployment lately. (GIGGLES) The whole thing's beginning to sound like a defense program.

MEREDITH: (HALF CRYING) Oh, jeepers, Frank! Don't argue with him! I wanna hear how you were a fireman.

MORGAN: Er—fireman! Oh, yes! After my rookie training, I was made driver of the fire engine, and you can imagine my excitement when my first alarm came in!

CONTE: Were you asleep, Frank?

MORGAN: Practically. But at the sound of the gong I was galvanized into action. The horses whinnied madly below, and I slipped into my shoes, slid down the shaft, slapped their shanks and shot from the shed like a shadow! (In the middle of a fire they give me tongue-twisters!)

MEREDITH: Never mind, Frank! Get to that fire!

MORGAN: It's coming! I whipped the frothing animals into a frenzy as we tore over the cobbled streets of Old Chicago, and it was only when my feet began to smoke that I realized I hadn't hitched the horses to the wagon.

CONTE: Fine fireman. Goes off without the engine!

MORGAN: Well, the horses should have known better anyway. We raced back to the firehouse, got into the harness and were on our way again in a trice. The call came from a barn on DeKoven and Jefferson Streets, where a cow, owned by a Mrs. O'Leary had kicked over a lantern. By the time I—

CONTE: Wait a minute!

MORGAN: The place was in a—

CONTE: Frank! That's the great Chicago Fire, and it happened October 8th, 1871, and you weren't even born, you faker!

MORGAN: Errr—born faker...eighteen seventy fire...errr—

CONTE: Well, it looks like you've shut yourself in a trap, Frank.

MORGAN: Oh—er—shut your trap, Frank...well—I—er—

CONTE: This is wonderful! And you can't get out of it because no matter how well preserved you are, you can't convince anybody you look seventy years old!

MEREDITH: He does, too! Go on, Frank!

MORGAN: Wait a minute!

CONTE: No, sir! Just tell us how you could attend that fire when it started in eighteen seventy-one!

MORGAN: Well, it smoldered for a long time! (GIGGLES) If he falls for that I'll get away with anything.

MEREDITH: Yes, sir, boy! We got him now, Frank! Huh, John, huh? What do you say, huh, John? Huh?

CONTE: Oh, stop it!

MORGAN: Keep going, Meredith, while I collect my wits!

CONTE: All right! So you drove the first fire engine to the great Chicago Fire!

MORGAN: I did? I mean, I did! Every piece of fire apparatus in the city was summoned to the scene, and because of my delay in harnessing the horses I was unable to be of any assistance.

CONTE: You mean you're not going to claim you put out the Chicago Fire single-handed!

MORGAN: No. Why should I lie about a thing that never happened?

CONTE: What!

MEREDITH: Well, pump my hose and call me Squirt!

MORGAN: Oh, dear. I can't stand around here any more and—

CONTE: Well, wait, Frank! You've gone so far with the story—you might as well finish it. You said you were present at the fire!

MORGAN: That's right.

CONTE: And you said you were driving a fire engine!

MORGAN: Quite so!

CONTE: Well, why couldn't you be of any assistance?

MORGAN: Well, the only available parking space was next to a fireplug and I didn't want to get a ticket! So long, fellows—I gotta buy some sunburn lotion.

MUSIC:	(APPLAUSE)
	MIDDLE COMMERCIAL-282 WORDS-1 MINUTE 37 SECONDS
CONTE:	Friends, how many of us can remember the first cup of coffee we ever tasted? Not many, I imagine, can recapture the first sensation of that wonderful, come-hither aroma…that exciting, stimulating flavor…the cheering warmth and life and goodness of that first cup of coffee.
	No, we can't do it for you. Can't give you back that first grand sensation. But what we can do for many of you is even better! We can give you a new coffee pleasure…new enjoyment…new appreciation of how good coffee can be. If you've never tasted it before, try your first cup of Maxwell House tomorrow. That's an experience I really envy you.
ANNOUNCER:	And it's the kind of experience more and more people are enjoying every day!
	Fifty years have rolled by since guests of the famous old Maxwell House began telling their friends to try its wonderful new coffee for a new experience in rare and mellow flavor. Today, Maxwell House Coffee is winning new friends faster than ever before in its history! Today, more stores sell Maxwell House than any other coffee in America!
	And no wonder. For never before has Maxwell House been so rich in those choice Highland grown coffees from Central and South America…coffees that give to this superb blend a rare, new fragrance…more deep down satisfying flavor…the full rounded body that makes you sit up and say, "Here is coffee."
	Best news of all…if it is news to you…Maxwell House sells at a price within everyone's reach. Won't you treat yourself to the extra pleasure that's yours in this superbly rich coffee…that's now…more than ever…good to the last drop!
MUSIC:	PLAY OFF
CONTE:	That was swell, Meredith. And now, ladies and—
SOUND:	PHONE RINGS
CONTE:	Hello.
STAFFORD:	(FILTER) Hello, John.
CONTE:	Hello, Daddy. Where are you?

STAFFORD:	I'm home. I don't think I'll be down tonight—I'm trying to finish up a picture I'm painting.
CONTE:	You paint pictures? I didn't know you were an artist.
STAFFORD:	My wife doesn't think so—but I've been at it for years. I really expect to do a good job on this new canvas.
CONTE:	Well, I wish you luck, Daddy. Stay out of Snooks' way.
STAFFORD:	She'll never find me tonight, old boy. So long, John.
CONTE:	Goodbye. (HANGS UP) If Snooks doesn't find him I'll eat the canvas.
MUSIC:	SNOOKS PLAY ON
FATHER:	I think I'd better put a little more umber on those clouds. Hmm… looks pretty good to me, boy! Yes, sir! I've finally found myself!
BRICE:	Was you lost, Daddy?
FATHER:	Snooks! How did you get down here?
BRICE:	I was hiding behind the furnace.
FATHER:	Leave my atelier at once!
BRICE:	Huh?
FATHER:	Get out of my studio!
BRICE:	This is the cellar, Daddy.
FATHER:	I know what it is—and if I choose to call it my studio I'll do so!
BRICE:	Why?
FATHER:	Because I do my painting down here.
BRICE:	Why are you wearing Mummy's dress?
FATHER:	It's not Mummy's dress—it's a smock! And the thing I have on my head is a beret!
BRICE:	Does Robespierre know you took it?
FATHER:	What has Robespierre got to do with my beret?
BRICE:	It looks like one of his old di—
FATHER:	Snooks! Robespierre never wore this on his head!
BRICE:	I know. He wore it on his—
FATHER:	That's beside the point! He doesn't use it any more and I made it into a beret! All artists wear a smock and beret.

BRICE:	Are you an artist, Daddy?
FATHER:	Yes, I am!
BRICE:	Well, why are you painting in the cellar?
FATHER:	Because I like to paint down here—and don't bother me with questions.
BRICE:	Last night you was painting in the kitchen.
FATHER:	I know! But I like to paint in the cellar better.
BRICE:	Why?
FATHER:	Because—because I get the north light down here. Besides, it gives me more the feeling of the true artist—cramped quarters, dreary-looking. Yes, it inspires me. Now, do you understand why I like to paint in the cellar?
BRICE:	Uh-huh…cause Mummy kicked you out of the kitchen.
FATHER:	Go on—rub salt in my wounds! Well, I won't stand for it much longer—I can tell you that! Some day your Mummy will wake up and find the worm has turned!
BRICE:	Ain't he the same at both ends?
FATHER:	Not this worm! Now, go away and let me paint in peace.
BRICE:	Shall I tell Mummy to let you paint in the kitchen, Daddy?
FATHER:	No, I'll suffer. All great artists painted under difficulties. Why, Rembrandt's greatest masterpiece was painted on an empty stomach.
BRICE:	Huh?
FATHER:	I said Rembrandt painted his most famous picture on an empty stomach.
BRICE:	Whose stomach did he paint it on, Daddy?
FATHER:	His own stomach!
BRICE:	Did it come off when he took a bath?
FATHER:	No!
BRICE:	Paint something on my stomach.
FATHER:	Snooks!
BRICE:	Paint something on my stomach!
FATHER:	Stop that or I'll color another part of your anatomy and you won't like it!

BRICE: Why?

FATHER: Just go upstairs and let me finish this picture.

BRICE: Can I see it, Daddy?

FATHER: No. You haven't got any more taste than your mother and you'll probably hurt my feelings.

BRICE: No, I won't.

FATHER: Well, all right. Here. This is my masterpiece.

BRICE: It's beautiful, Daddy.

FATHER: You—really like it?

BRICE: I love it.

FATHER: There! A child judges art instinctively! Of course she likes it! Does it look real, darling?

BRICE: Uh-huh. It makes me very hungry.

FATHER: Hungry? Why should this painting make you hungry? It's supposed to be a beautiful sunset.

BRICE: Oh, I thought it was a fried egg.

FATHER: Ahhh! What do you know about art! That picture will make history when it's exhibited.

BRICE: Are you gonna sell it, Daddy?

FATHER: No. I only painted it for my own amusement.

BRICE: (LAUGHS)

FATHER: What are you laughing at?

BRICE: I think it's funny, too.

FATHER: Well, I don't care what you think. Go away and let me work.

BRICE: No, I wanna stay here.

FATHER: Then sit in the corner and play.

BRICE: What shall I do, Daddy?

FATHER: Do nothing.

BRICE: How will I know when I'm finished?

FATHER: Here! Take this crayon and draw something on a piece of paper.

BRICE: What shall I draw?

FATHER: Anything, only don't bother me. Hmm...I'll have to highlight this

	sunset a little better. Does kind of look like a fried egg up close. I'll touch it up with a little ochre—very steady—very careful—
BRICE:	Daddy!
FATHER:	Snooks! You made me smudge my painting! What do you want?
BRICE:	How many kinds of milk is there?
FATHER:	I don't know—five or six, I guess. There's buttermilk, whole milk, skim milk—err—
BRICE:	Milk of Magnesia?
FATHER:	No. Why do you want to know how many kinds of milk there are?
BRICE:	I'm drawing a picture of a cow.
FATHER:	Well?
BRICE:	I wanna know how many faucets to put on it.
FATHER:	Listen, if you annoy me once more you'll go right upstairs!
BRICE:	Well, show me some more pictures.
FATHER:	No!
BRICE:	I wanna see that picture with the towel on it.
FATHER:	No. You can't see that.
BRICE:	Why?
FATHER:	Because—it's not the type of picture little girls are interested in.
BRICE:	Why?
FATHER:	I tell you it wouldn't interest little girls!
BRICE:	How about little boys?
FATHER:	Just forget about that picture and leave it covered with the towel.
BRICE:	I wanna see it.
FATHER:	Leave it alone! Here—I'll show you a nice picture I painted. Look at this.
BRICE:	What is it?
FATHER:	This is a wonderful sea study. I call it "Faith."
BRICE:	Why?
FATHER:	Because that's the theme. See that little boat being tossed by the waves? And do you notice the sailor on board with his hands raised in supplication? He has faith that he'll be rescued.

BRICE: What's faith, Daddy?

FATHER: Well, you can see the boat and you can see the sailor—but if I told you it was a woman and she was standing on a coffee can, and you believed me, that would be faith. Understand?

BRICE: Understand.

FATHER: All right—what is faith?

BRICE: A woman on a can.

FATHER: That's closer than I expected. Well, anyway—how do you like the picture?

BRICE: No good.

FATHER: What's the matter with it?

BRICE: I wanna see the other one with the towel on it.

FATHER: I told you I won't let you…Snooks! Come away from that easel!

BRICE: I wanna look!

FATHER: Don't touch that towel or I'll—

BRICE: Oooooooooooooh, Daddy.

FATHER: All right, you little snooper! You pulled off the towel! So you saw the picture! What of it!

BRICE: She's fat, ain't she?

FATHER: The artistic word is buxom. At least that's what they say in the best places.

BRICE: Well, in the best places she's—

FATHER: Never mind about that. And you might as well understand that it's no crime for an artist to paint the human form without clothing.

BRICE: It looks like my teacher, Daddy.

FATHER: Well, it's not your teacher.

BRICE: Why?

FATHER: Because your teacher doesn't look like that!

BRICE: How do you know?

FATHER: Just cover it up—and forget you ever saw it. And if you're thinking of telling your Mummy anything—I copied it from a book!

BRICE: I won't say nothing, Daddy, if—if—

FATHER: If what?

BRICE:	If you show me the book.	
FATHER:	No! I'm not going to let you browbeat me!	
BRICE:	Then I'll take the picture up to Mummy!	
FATHER:	Snooks! Come back here! Drop that picture!	
SOUND:	CRASH AND RIP	
BRICE:	I think I'll go now.	
FATHER:	Ohhh! You've ruined it! The canvas is mutilated!	
BRICE:	Only half of it, Daddy.	
FATHER:	(BITTERLY) Only half!	
BRICE:	The good half's all right.	
FATHER:	Well, I'm going to teach you a lesson! Turn over! (WHACK) There!	
BRICE:	Waaahhh!	
FATHER:	And there! (WHACK) There! (WHACK)	
BRICE:	Waaahhh! Don't spank me any more!	
FATHER:	All right. You know you deserved it though, don't you?	
BRICE:	Huh?	
FATHER:	Tell me why I spanked you…I want to know why I spanked you!	
BRICE:	That's just the trouble.	
FATHER:	What's the trouble?	
BRICE:	First you spank me, then you don't know why you done it!	
FATHER:	Ahhh—baloney!	
BRICE:	Waahahhh!	
MUSIC:	(APPLAUSE)	

COMMERCIAL: CLOSING COMMERCIAL-154 WORDS-52 SECONDS

ANNOUNCER: Friends…we can promise you extra flavor…extra enjoyment in every pound of Maxwell House Coffee you buy. But that's not all!

You can buy as many pounds of Maxwell House at a time as you like…and be sure the coffee in the last can will be just as fresh and delicious as the first! Now, these days, it's important to remember not every coffee can make that promise!

	For, unlike ordinary coffees, Maxwell House is taken, fresh and fragrant from the roasting ovens, and packed in the familiar blue super vacuum can. All air is first removed. Then the can is sealed under a vacuum. No air can get it, so no flavor can get out. That famous blue can brings Maxwell House to you not days fresh…but roaster fresh…always!
	So, why not stock up with one of the truly good things in life! Put Maxwell House on your shopping list…tomorrow!
MUSIC:	PLAY OFF
MUSIC:	THEME—PLAYS FOR:
CONTE:	Which leaves us just about enough time to tell you that we'll all be back again next Thursday evening at Maxwell House Coffee Time. Fanny Brice as Baby Snooks, Frank Morgan, who appears with us through the courtesy of Metro-Goldwyn-Mayer, Hanley Stafford, and Meredith Willson.
	Until next Thursday then, this is John Conte, saying goodnight and good luck from the makers of Maxwell House…the coffee that's always…good to the last drop!
MUSIC:	(APPLAUSE)
ANNOUNCER:	A girl of eighteen steps innocently into a house full of intrigue, and Kate Hopkins looks on, suddenly realizing that she, too, and her son in uniform, will play vital parts in a strange battle for one man's love.
	Tune in tomorrow to "Kate Hopkins," the dramatic story of life under the tropical skies of a Louisiana plantation. Remember, "The Story of Kate Hopkins," one of radio's truly great stories, brought to you every day over another network by Maxwell House Coffee.
	THIS IS THE NATIONAL BROADCASTING COMPANY

AS BROADCAST
MAXWELL HOUSE COFFEE TIME
JANUARY 7, 1943

1. OPENING

2. THEME...CAST INTRO

"FOR ME AND MY GAL"

3. MORGAN SPOT

4. MIDDLE COMMERCIAL

5. "DEARLY BELOVED"

6. BABY SNOOKS SPOT

7. CLOSING COMMERCIAL

8. THEME...SIGN OFF

9. HITCH-HIKE

(ON CUE)

BRICE:	Daddy!
STAFF:	Don't bother me, Snooks! I have checks to make out! Look at these doctor bills!
BRICE:	What are they for, daddy?
STAFF:	The twins—they cost me a fortune. I've already made four payments—and this is the last.
BRICE:	Then do we own them?
STAFF:	Yes. What's this bill here?...Oh, yes—my lumbago.
BRICE:	Did the doctor bring that, too, daddy?
STAFF:	No! You remember when I had lumbago—my back swelled up and I couldn't move.
BRICE:	Yeah.
STAFF:	Well, this bill is the fee for the doctor's house call.

BRICE:	Do you have to pay it now?
STAFF:	Yes.
BRICE:	Why?
STAFF:	Because it's back swell house call fee time.
BRICE:	Ohhh! daddy.

(APPLAUSE...THEME)

HARLOW: Yes, ladies and gentlemen, it's Maxwell House Coffee time—as if you didn't understand daddy! So prepare for another pleasant half hour with Frank Morgan, the Maxwell House orchestra conducted by Frank Tours, Hanley Stafford in his paternal role, and Fanny Brice as radio's original problem child—the one and only Baby Snooks. And now here is our master of ceremonies—your host for the evening—John Conte!

"FOR ME AND MY GAL" – CONTE & ORCH.

(APPLAUSE)

CONTE: Thank you, ladies and gentlemen, and good evening. Even the most casual observer has noticed that during any national crisis or emergency the nation's leaders become alphabetically inclined. There's the O.P.A.—O.E.M.—W.P.N., and all the rest of the hard-working and efficient government agencies.

TOURS: I say, John, that's a very profound observation.

CONTE: It is? What's profound about it, Frank?

TOURS: Well, it appears to me there's some sort of symbolism involved. Clear case of something or other, don't you think?

CONTE: Something or other.

TOURS: Has a scientific name, of course, but I don't suppose you'd know what it is and I don't wish to be pedantic.

CONTE: Oh. Do you know the scientific name?

TOURS: No.

CONTE: Tours, I must confess I have great difficulty following your reasoning.

TOURS: Think nothing of it, old boy—I frequently have the same trouble myself. Once made a remark that baffled me for eleven weeks.

CONTE: I see. Well, our guest this evening—ladies & gentlemen will be—

TOURS: Guest? Another one?

CONTE: What do you mean another one?

TOURS:	You had one last week, John. Gets quite monotonous, you know. Barely enough time left for the musical portion of—
CONTE:	I told you, Frank, that the music plays a very small part on our program. We're interested mainly in the quality and not the quantity.
TOURS:	Is that so? Well, if it's quality you're after, how do you explain away this Morgan chap?
CONTE:	Morgan chap. He's one of the greatest comedians in the world, that's all!
TOURS:	Can't say I subscribe to that at all.
CONTE:	Well, I haven't got time to argue because our guest is a very important gentleman and it's time I presented him. He represents the O.W.I.
TOURS:	That sounds very impressive. What does it mean?
CONTE:	It's the Office of War Information. And, ladies and gentlemen, it's a privilege to introduce to you the Acting Deputy Chief of the O.W.I's Domestic Radio Bureau—Mr. Cornwell Jackson. Mr. Jackson, if you please.
	(APPLAUSE)
CORNY:	Thank you.
CONTE:	I may add, ladies and gentlemen, that I've known Mr. Jackson for many years and that he's intimately known to his friends as Corny. Isn't that right, Corny?
CORNY:	Unfortunately yes—And, John, I wish you'd try to make it sound more like a noun and less like an adjective.
TOURS:	Touchy, isn't he?
CONTE:	He isn't touchy, Frank—it's just that the word corny is a derogatory term used among musicians, as you know.
TOURS:	Didn't know it at all, John. Are you certain of that?
CONTE:	Quite sure. You mean you've never come across the word corny?
TOURS:	Very often. My fan mail's full of it. I shall have to burn the stuff from now on.
CONTE:	Fine. Corny, as I understand it, the true function of your department is to disseminate war information to the public, withholding as little of the vital facts as possible, without giving aid or comfort to the enemy. Is that it?

CORNY: In a nutshell, yes. But the O.W.I. covers a lot of ground. Thru the wonderful co-operation of radio, and I mean everybody connected with radio, we've managed to launch several drives that have attained almost unheard of results.

CONTE: You mean things like the war bonds campaign, fuel conservation, Junior Red Cross and so forth?

CORNY: Among other things. Right now we're in the midst of one of the greatest campaigns of all.

CONTE: What's that?

CORNY: Security of war information.

CONTE: That means keep your eyes open and your ears open, but keep your mouth closed?

TOURS: Oh, I say, that's preposterous. Chap has to yawn once in a while. You know, particularly during these dull interviews.

CONTE: Don't be se literal, Tours! Mr. Jackson just means that it's all right to see and hear things—but not repeat them. Go sit down, will you, Frank.

CONTE: Certainly.

TOURS: Thank you. I find this very fatiguing anyway. (HE BLOWS)

CORNY: Of course John, you can talk about anything you hear on the radio—or read in the newspapers...But bits of war information you pick up at your job or learn from anyone in the armed forces—no matter how harmless they may sound—they should be kept strictly to yourself. Remember—in this war men's lives depend on surprise and surprise depends on secrecy.

CONTE: That's that. Tell me, Corny, do you honestly believe that a chance remark, innocently spoken, can cause a great catastrophe?

CORNY: Definitely.

MORGAN: (COMING IN) And how! I just said "Hello babe" to a buxom lass in the hall and her husband clipped me so bad—

CONTE: Frank!

MORGAN: Hello, fellows. Are my front teeth missing or have I got my tongue caught in a life-saver?

CONTE: What happened?

MORGAN: I don't know. I'm still dizzy from a sneak punch delivered by a punchy sneak!

CONTE:	It's your own fault for accosting strange girls!
MORGAN:	There was nothing strange about this girl at all, Jockey. She looked just like all the other girls I say hello to.
CONTE:	Why don't you admit you're a masher instead of trying to hedge, hog.
MORGAN:	Oh, hedgehog. This is Thankless Thursday and it's hedgehog—meatless Tuesday it's the porcupine for (SHAKES HIS HEAD)—That doesn't sound like me at all. I think I'd better take it on the lam.
CONTE:	Oh, stop beefing.
MORGAN:	Well, that butchered everything. Where's the dame you made your chance remark to, Jockey?
CONTE:	No dames! The chance remark you chanced to hear indicated loose words that the enemy turns into vital information. We've all got to clam up on troop movements, war plant work and things like that.
MORGAN:	That's a very sensible idea. And if I were you I'd keep mum right now, my boy.
CONTE:	Why?
MORGAN:	Come here…(LOWERS VOICE)…That pug-ugly alongside of you looks like a spy.
CONTE:	Spy!
MORGAN:	Shhh!
CORNY:	I beg you pardon, sir! I overheard that remark!
MORGAN:	See! Eavesdropping already!
CONTE:	What's the matter with you, Frank. This man's not a spy!
CORNY:	No—I'm Cornwell Jackson, O.W.I.
MORGAN:	Well, how do you do, sir—I'm Frank Morgan, MGM.
CORNY:	I'm very glad to know you—I think.
MORGAN:	Oh. Are they making many pictures at your studio, son?
CORNY:	I'm not in pictures, Mr. Morgan.
MORGAN:	That's very obvious. And I can think of several good reasons why—but I haven't got the time.
CONTE:	Frank! OWI stands for the Office of War Information, and Mr. Cornwell Jackson is Acting Deputy Chief, if you please!

MORGAN: Err—information please…Warjack…Yes. Well, Mr. Popcorn—

CORNY: Jackson. Cornwell Jackson.

MORGAN: Yes. Your name has been brought to my attention but in the press of other urgent matters I haven't been able to act on your promotion. However, I assure—

CONTE: Wait a minute! Hold it! Just a second, are you implying that you belong to some government agency, Morgan?

MORGAN: (LAUGHS) Are you serious, Jockey?

CONTE: Yes, he is serious

MORGAN: My movements are shielded by great secrecy, of course—

CONTE: Of course.

MORGAN: Of course. But since its inception I've been head of the N.T.U.—also chief of the S.T.U.—and now that both agencies are merged you can readily understand what that means.

CONTE: What?

MORGAN: N.U.T.S.T.U. It's a cumbersome set of letters, but they have more significance than you think.

CORNY: What sort of work is your department engaged in, Mr. Morgan?

MORGAN: Counter-espionage—but confined strictly to apprehending beautiful female spies who operate in the guise of chorines, artists' models and cover girls.

CONTE: Tough work.

MORGAN: It's grueling—in a delightful sort of way. (LAUGHS) But no sacrifice is too great where one's country is concerned. Isn't that right, Mr. Jackpot?

CORNY: Jackson.

MORGAN: Yes. I have to suffer the slings and arrows of my carping critics when I'm seen in various cafes with a beauty on each arm—but my work is so confidential I can't even explain to my wife.

CORNY: Naturally you can't explain—this is wartime!

MORGAN: Well, I couldn't even explain in peacetime, but that's beside the point.

CONTE: Frank, how is it your department only goes after female spies?

MORGAN: That's a natural question, my boy—and I wish it didn't have such an unnatural answer.

CORNY:	Have you managed to PINCH any of these glamorous spies, Mr. Morgan?
MORGAN:	Well, some of them are friendlier than others, but they all let—Oh! PINCHED! You mean have I nabbed any yet?
CORNY:	That's right.
MORGAN:	Err—that's a military secret.
CONTE:	Oh, sure. Where did you get the training for this dangerous job of yours, Frank?
MORGAN:	It all dates back to the time I was employed in the Treasury Department as a spotter, with headquarters at the Mint.
CORNY:	Oh, you were a Mint spy.
MORGAN:	Mince pie. Amazing what you can get a guest to say. But every day for three months a stack of hundred dollar bills would disappear. A careful check was made of the serial numbers, and then began a chase that took me all over the world.
CONTE:	Where did they catch you?
MORGAN:	In Paris, But I'd already blown most of the dough on those French—what am I saying?
CONTE:	I'm sorry, Frank. I meant to say did you catch the culprit?
MORGAN:	Well, that's different. When I started the manhunt, the trail was already cold, and I arrived in Brussels, with not a single clue. I immediately went to work combing the bistros, cleaning out the dens, and scouring the alleys.
CORNY:	What for?
MORGAN:	I had a side job with the street cleaning department. A call from my immediate superior brought me post-haste to Hastepost, that's a small hamlet in Denmark. Upon discovering I'd made no progress, he immediately began to wax wroth. Roth, in turn, waxed him, then they both waxed me and we slid out of town without a sound. (I think I'm skidding, fellows).
CONTE:	Then you never caught the crook?
MORGAN:	Patience, my boy. As soon as I returned to the United States, a hot tip led me to the Hopi Indian Reservation at Minneapolis. I—
CONTE:	Minneapolis! You're insane—the Hopi tribe inhabits only the northern part of Arizona!
MORGAN:	Oh—only. Hopi…Hopi get out of this one.

CONTE: Well, you're nailed now, weasel.

MORGAN: Ridiculous! I can show you proof of my visit to the reservation, because the chief gave us each a keepsake.

CONTE: What?

MORGAN: My superior got a braided night-stick and for doing so well I got a beaded sap...Well, I gotta beat it, sap.

CONTE: Come back here! Frank, what about this reservation—and why should you go there anyway?

MORGAN: To solve the mystery. I was after a certain brave who had just been discharged by the Treasury Department.

CORNY: Why did the Treasury hire the Indian in the first place?

MORGAN: As a model. He was supposed to get his head on five million nickels.

CONTE: Well?

MORGAN: Instead of that, he got his hands on five thousand dollars. Well, I'll see you later, fellows. I gotta do a little spying.

(MUSIC...APPLAUSE)

MIDDLE COMMERCIAL

(ORCHESTRA STARTS PLAYING "MARY, IT'S A GRAND OLD NAME" IN HORRIBLE TUNE AND BALANCE, THEN....)

CONTE: Frank! Frank Tours! What are you doing?

(ORCHESTRA FADES DOWN AND OUT, FLATLY)

CONTE: What *were* you doing?

TOURS: Merely conducting a bit of an experiment.

CONTE: Experiment?

(START COMMERCIAL TIME HERE) 196 words 1 min: 8 sec. plus 18 sec. music

TOURS: Yes, y'know, our friend Wilcox here is always talking about blends...both musical and Maxwell House. So I was merely demonstrating what a really *bad* blend would *sound* like.

WILCOX: And it would *taste* just as bad. Now, Frank, let's do a musical blend with all the skill that goes into the blending of Maxwell House Coffee. First now we must have *mellowness*...

TOURS: For that, the woodwinds…

(WOODWINDS AS DIRECTED … THREE SECONDS)

WILCOX: And *richness*…

TOURS: The strings…

(STRINGS AS DIRECTED … THREE SECONDS)

WILCOX: And *full-body*…

TOURS: The rhythm section…

(RHYTHM AS DIRECTED…THREE SECONDS)

WILCOX: And *vigorous flavor*…

TOURS: The brasses…

(BRASSES AS DIRECTED…THREE SECONDS)

MIDDLE COMMERCIAL CONTINUED

WILCOX: Yes, mellowness…richness…full-body…vigorous flavor…all skillfully combined into a smooth beautiful blend…

(ORCHESTRA REAL JOB, LAST FOUR BARS…SIX SECONDS)

WILCOX: Yes, friends…skill in blending is just as important to the coffee you drink as it is to the music you hear. So when you buy coffee, won't you remember the skill of the Maxwell House experts? For years they've been producing and improving a blend *so well-liked* it has made Maxwell House the choice of millions who prefer truly *good* coffee! And since all of us are getting along with less coffee these days, certainly you'll want the extra enjoyment skillfully-blended Maxwell House brings! For now, as always, Maxwell House Coffee is…Good to the *Last Drop!*

(PLAY OFF)

CONTE: That was delightful, Frank. And now, ladies and —

(PHONE RINGS)

CONTE: Excuse me…Hello.

STAFF: (FILTER) Hello, John.

CONTE: Hello, daddy. Coming down this evening?

STAFF: Can't leave tonight. I'm on the verge of my greatest discovery.

CONTE:	Are you inventing again? What is it this time?
STAFF:	There's a shortage of dairy products, isn't there, John?
CONTE:	Yes, but—
STAFF:	Just wait and see what comes out of my laboratory. Goodbye, John!
CONTE:	Goodbye, daddy. (HANGS UP) If anything comes out of his laboratory, I'll bet it'll be Baby Snooks!
	(SNOOKS PLAY-ON)
FATHER:	(GLOATING) Ha, ha. Nobody'll ever believe it. A synthetic dairy farm! Oceans of milk—tons of butter! All from my fertile brain!
BRICE:	Hello, daddy!
FATHER:	Snooks! Don't cross that threshold!
BRICE:	Why?
FATHER:	I've forbidden you time and again to enter my laboratory while I'm working! And now I'm telling you for the last time.
BRICE:	Well, I'm glad of that, daddy. I got sick and tired of hearing you tell me not—
FATHER:	I mean this is final! Go right back to your room and go to sleep.
BRICE:	I can't sleep, daddy.
FATHER:	You can too! You're just looking for an excuse to come down here and pester me.
BRICE:	Oh, no, daddy.
FATHER:	Then why don't you go to sleep?
BRICE:	'Cause I wanna see what you're doing.
FATHER:	Very well—I'll tell you what I'm doing. Come in and close the door…(DOOR CLOSES)…You see that liquid in the test-tube?
BRICE:	Uh-huh.
FATHER:	That's milk.
BRICE:	Huh?
FATHER:	That's milk. M-I-L-K—milk.
BRICE:	It's green, daddy.
FATHER:	Well, it does have a greenish tinge, yes.
BRICE:	Did it come from a green cow?

FATHER: It didn't come from a cow at all. I made it.

BRICE: (WORRIED) Let's leave the door open, daddy.

FATHER: Don't stare at me like I'm crazy! I know what I'm doing! I made that milk in this laboratory—and what's more, I can produce a hundred gallons of it in two minutes!

BRICE: Is that why mummy calls you busy?

FATHER: Never mind what mummy calls me! I make it out of sink water and a couple of inexpensive ingredients. Of course, I haven't got the proper color yet—but that's a triviality. It's milk, all right—it tastes like milk, too. Go on—taste it.

BRICE: No.

FATHER: Why not?

BRICE: It don't smell good.

FATHER: Well, maybe I put a little too much sulfur in it—but I wanted to kill the taste of the carbolic acid.

BRICE: Who told you how to make it, daddy?

FATHER: Nobody told me. I invented it myself. Do you know what cow's milk is composed of?

BRICE: Uh-huh.

FATHER: Are you sure?

BRICE: Uh-huh.

FATHER: Well, what is it composed of?

BRICE: I dunno.

FATHER: I thought not. Well, milk is composed of eighty-seven percent water, four percent fat, five percent lactose, three percent caseinogen, one percent lactalbumin, and two percent salts.

BRICE: Ain't there any milk in it at all?

FATHER: Look, altogether it makes milk. And each of these things you can buy at a drugstore.

BRICE: How do the cows get thru the door?

FATHER: They don't. Cows have a different way of getting the ingredients. They get it from their fodder.

BRICE: Do bulls give milk?

FATHER: Of course not!

BRICE:	Well, ain't a bull a cow's father.
FATHER:	I said fodder not father! The stuff they eat turns to milk.
BRICE:	Why?
FATHER:	It's a complicated physical process. But I said to myself that there couldn't possibly be any more stupid animal than a cow, isn't that right?
BRICE:	Is it?
FATHER:	Yes. Well, my conclusion was that if a cow could produce milk so could I! It stands to reason that I can do anything a cow can do.
BRICE:	Can you brush a fly off your hind legs?
FATHER:	I haven't got any hind legs! And I can brush flies off just like a cow!
BRICE:	With your tail?
FATHER:	You're just getting technical! I accomplish the same result—only I execute it in a different way. That's how I went about getting milk.
BRICE:	Only it came out green.
FATHER:	That's right.
BRICE:	And it smells like kerosene.
FATHER:	It does not! It smells like creosote.
BRICE:	Why did you make it, daddy?
FATHER:	Because there's a terrific shortage of dairy products. You know it's almost impossible to get butter, don't you?
BRICE:	We got plenty of butter, daddy.
FATHER:	We have not! They'll only sell you a quarter of a pound!
BRICE:	Yeah—but me and mummy went to forty stores yesterday and we got a quarter of a pound at each one.
FATHER:	That's downright unpatriotic! What did she do that for?
BRICE:	Mummy said she wanted to get some before the hoarders got it all.
FATHER:	But it wasn't necessary—I've already made synthetic butter from my artificial milk.
BRICE:	Is it that purple stuff on the bench?
FATHER:	Yes. I think that's the butter—I made cheese, too. One of these slabs is butter.
BRICE:	One is purple and one is red.

FATHER:	Don't worry so much about the colors! One is cheese and one is butter—I know that much. Here, taste a little piece of this.
BRICE:	No—you taste it.
FATHER:	Oh, go on! You don't think I want to poison you, do you?... Do you?
BRICE:	Uh-huh.
FATHER:	Don't be silly. Take a tiny little taste. Just put it on your tongue. Go on.
BRICE:	Awight…(SPITS IT OUT)…Oh, daddy!
FATHER:	Well, is it the cheese or the butter?
BRICE:	It tastes like castor oil.
FATHER:	It does? Well, that's the cheese. The butter tastes like quinine. It isn't so bad, is it, Snooks?
BRICE:	It's awful, daddy.
FATHER:	Well, I guess I still—
	(CHICKEN CACKLES)
BRICE:	What's that, daddy?
FATHER:	Oh, I—er—I have a chicken back there in a cage.
BRICE:	Why?
FATHER:	Well, I—er—Snooks.
BRICE:	Yes, daddy.
FATHER:	Don't repeat this to anybody—promise me.
BRICE:	I promise, daddy.
FATHER:	Well—I've been studying the habits of a laying hen. And—well—
BRICE:	You ain't gonna lay an egg, are you, daddy?
FATHER:	Don't be silly. But I do have hopes of producing an egg without the aid of the chicken. (HOPEFULLY) It isn't entirely beyond the realm of possibility, do you think, Snooks?
BRICE:	Oh no, daddy. If a chicken can do it without you, why can't you do it without the chicken?
FATHER:	That's brilliant reasoning. You know I'm so thankful for your encouragement, Snooks. You don't know what it does to a man to work by himself night after night.

BRICE:	I think I know, daddy.
FATHER:	Yes. Well, I've got this hen in a cage, and she's laid three or four eggs. They're going to hatch pretty soon.
BRICE:	Are they?
FATHER:	I think so. Would you like to see how the little chicks come out of the eggs?
BRICE:	No. I wanna see how they get in.
FATHER:	Now, don't spoil everything! I'm going to let you watch me duplicate a hen's egg.
BRICE:	How will you make the shells, daddy?
FATHER:	That's the problem. It's simple enough to make the white and the yolk, but I still haven't invented a way to enclose the stuff in a shell.
BRICE:	Why don't you buy some eggs, blow out the insides and then stuff 'em?
FATHER:	You can't buy eggs.
BRICE:	Why?
FATHER:	Why? Why do you think I'm inventing them? There's a shortage!
BRICE:	Well—why don't you just make *scrambled* eggs?
FATHER:	Too messy. I've got to make the real thing.
BRICE:	How does the *chicken* do it?
FATHER:	It's a miracle of simplicity. That's what drives me crazy. Now, just look at this hen…(CHICKEN CACKLES SOFTLY)…She looks like an ordinary chicken, doesn't she?
BRICE:	Uh-huh.
FATHER:	Well, she isn't. She's sensitive to colors. What would you say if I told you I was able to make this hen lay an egg of any color I pleased?
BRICE:	I would say open the door, daddy—I'm going to bed.
FATHER:	Wait a minute! It's true, yesterday I inadvertently covered her cage with a brown cloth—and she laid a brown egg.
BRICE:	Imagine that.
FATHER:	That's not all. The day before I placed a sheet of white paper near her and what do you think?

BRICE: And she laid a white egg.

FATHER: You've guessed it. If you don't believe me, wait here and I'll fetch the eggs.

BRICE: I'll wait, daddy…(CHICKEN CLUCKS SOFTLY)…I think daddy's fooling me, Mrs. Chicken. I'll bet you can't lay no colored eggs…(CHICKEN CLUCKS)…Where's that stuff?…Now, let's see what happens. Come on—eat it! Eat it or I'll choke you! Eat it. Eat it.

(A SERIES OF THE GODDAMDEST CHICKEN NOISES…LOUD POP)

FATHER: Snooks! What was that noise?

BRICE: It was the chicken, daddy. I wanted her to lay a colored egg, so I showed her your green milk and your purple cheese and your red butter.

FATHER: But she looks like she's dead!

BRICE: Yeah—I think she exploded trying to make good.

FATHER: You little—(SOCK)

BRICE: Waaaaaaaaaaaahhhhhh!

(MUSIC…APPLAUSE)

CLOSING COMMERCIAL

WILCOX: At this time, a word to the ladies in charge of their family's ration coupons, each good for the purchase of one pound of coffee.

Since Monday last, when the second ration period started, no doubt many of you have turned in coupon number twenty-eight. All of us hope, of course, that you remembered to ask for Maxwell House Coffee…as mellow-rich, delicious and satisfying as ever!

If your grocer by chance had no Maxwell House, ask for it again the next time you shop. It's worth the slight delay to get this delightful coffee.

But ladies—even Maxwell House Coffee must be made right if you expect to enjoy its full flavor and strength. So follow brewing directions printed on the Maxwell House label. This way you'll get the best in Maxwell House Coffee goodness—economically, too.

You'll find it pays…more than ever, *these* days—to get *truly good* coffee. So every time you turn in a ration coupon for a pound of coffee, remember to make it—*Maxwell House* coffee!

	(THEME)
MUSIC:	THEME…FADES FOR
CONTE:	Which rings down the curtain for tonight, ladies and gentlemen, until next Thursday evening at Maxwell House Coffee Time…. when we return with Fanny Brice as Baby Snooks, Frank Morgan who appears with us thru the courtesy of Metro-Goldwyn-Mayer, Hanley Stafford, Frank Tours and Harlow Wilcox.

                Maxwell House Coffee Time is written by Phil Rapp.

                By the way, tomorrow evening, listen to "The Adventures of the Thin Man." Formerly heard Wednesday, hereafter every Friday… over another network. See your paper for time and station.

                This is John Conte, saying goodnight and good luck from the makers of Maxwell House. Frank Morgan will next be seen in "Mr. Justice Goes Hunting." And friends, now that you're going to drink your coffee down to the last drop, wouldn't it be smart to buy Maxwell House—the coffee that's always—good to the last drop.

MAXWELL HOUSE COFFEE TIME
APRIL 2, 1942

1. SNOOKS & DADDY OPENER
2. THEME....CAST INTRO.
3. FRANK MORGAN SPOT
4. COMMERCIAL
5. "A GARDENIA IN MY BUTTONHOLE"
6. BABY SNOOKS SPOT
7. COMMERCIAL
8. FABLE
9. SIGNOFF
10. HITCH-HIKE

BRICE: Daddy!
FATHER: Snooks, I thought you were going to sit quietly and read your picture book.
BRICE: I wanna ask you something.
FATHER: All right—quick. What is it?
BRICE: What's this funny thing with the long tail and the little hands?
FATHER: That's a kangaroo. He's a native of Australia.
BRICE: Is that what they look like?
FATHER: Certainly.
BRICE: Then why did Aunt Penny marry one of those?
FATHER: What?
BRICE: You said Aunt Penny married a native of Austral —
FATHER: She married an Australian! Not a kangaroo!
BRICE: Why?

FATHER:	How do I know. Read your book.
BRICE:	Wait a minute, daddy. Is this a goat?
FATHER:	Goat!
BRICE:	Yeah, goat.
FATHER:	Snooks! Look at those antlers—does that look like a goat?
BRICE:	I dunno.
FATHER:	Besides, the name is written right on the bottom of the page. D-E-E-R! What does that spell?
BRICE:	Lion?
FATHER:	No! What does mummy sometimes call me?
BRICE:	Oh. I didn't know a donkey had horns.
FATHER:	It's a deer! A buck! That's a male deer.
BRICE:	I thought a buck was a dollar.
FATHER:	A buck is slang for a dollar. So is a bean—or a frogskin—or a smacker. An ill-bred person might say, "My hat cost five smackers."
BRICE:	How many smackers did your shoes cost, daddy?
FATHER:	Eight smackers.
BRICE:	Eight smackers what?
FATHER:	Eight smackers well House Coffee Time. Read your book.
	(MUSIC...APPLAUSE)
HARLOW:	Yes, ladies and gentlemen, it's Maxwell House Coffee Time as you have no doubt deciphered for yourself. And that means Frank Morgan, Meredith Wilson and his music, Hanley Stafford as Daddy, and Fanny Brice's characterization of the madcap moppet - the one and only Baby Snooks! Now, here is our master of ceremonies - your host for the evening—John Conte!
	(APPLAUSE)
	SONG: CONTE & ORCH.
	(APPLAUSE)
CONTE:	Thank you, ladies and gentlemen—and good evening. In these hectic times the national ear seems turned to the news commentators and analysts that help enlighten us thru the medium of the various radio networks. Broadcasting regularly from the Warner Brothers station KFWB here in Hollywood is one of the most

	unusual and well-informed war experts of them all. I refer to the eminent Dr. H.H. Chang, a gentlemen who is as respected in diplomatic circles as—well—as much as Meredith Willson is in musical circles.
MERE:	Gee, this is interesting.
CONTE:	I thought that'd get you. At any rate, I won't bore you with a long biographical sketch of this renowned interpreter of world affairs—since I'm sure you're all as anxious to hear him speak as we are. So, ladies and gentlemen, may I say we feel privileged and proud to present one of the most outstanding representatives of an outstanding race of hard-fighting people - the brilliant Chinese scholar—Dr. H. H. Chang. Dr. Chang!
	(APPLAUSE)
CHANG:	Thank you, Mr. Conte. Your introduction was most flattering.
CONTE:	On the contrary, doctor. I left a great deal unsaid.
CHANG:	Not a great deal—just one thing. And at the risk of being considered forward, I should like to say it. May I?
MERE:	Pray do.
CHANG:	Thank you, Mr. Willson. For the benefit of nobody but myself I want to add to Mr. Conte's gracious introduction that my program is to be heard every Monday, Wednesday, and Friday at exactly six fifteen P.M.
CONTE:	Well done, doctor. And for the benefit of the uninitiated I would like to add that your addition is technically known in radio parlance as a plug.
CHANG:	An admirable word—and very expressive. But the thought itself was covered centuries ago by the great Chinese philosopher Hsu Hsieh, who so aptly said—(CHINESE SPEECH)
MERE:	He said that, huh? What does it mean, doctor?
CHANG:	Loosely translated, it means "Them as has, gits."
MERE:	Jeepers! We been saying that in Mason City for years!
CONTE:	There you are, Meredith! And you never suspected that you had a grain of Chinese philosophy in your body!
MERE:	Just shows you how a thing gets around. Them as has, gits. Hmmph!
CHANG:	Mr. Willson is jesting, of course.
CONTE:	Oh, of course.

CHANG: He's quite a wit, isn't he?

CONTE: Well, you're half right, anyway. Now, doctor, I'd like you to answer a few questions. You recently arrived here from Chungking, didn't you?

CHANG: Yes.

CONTE: Are you on a special mission? The reason I ask is because I know you were the former Chinese minister to Portugal, Poland and Czechoslovakia.

CHANG: What a subtle way you have of bringing out dull facts, Mr. Conte. No, I'm not on a special mission—although I've just accepted the invitation to be Director of the China Institute.

MERE: China Institute? Say, doc, Peggy wants a new set of dishes and I—

CONTE: Meredith! He's not selling dishes!

MERE: Oh.

CHANG: No, Mr. Willson, the China I'm referring to has nothing in common with dishes—and it's infinitely harder to break.

CONTE: Excellent, doctor. I think Hirohito's already discovered that.

CHANG: If he hasn't, he will. Proceed with your questions, Mr. Conte.

CONTE: Yes. Among your biographical notes I find this item. "Dr. Chang is the only diplomat that ever lectured before the Warsaw Academy of Science." Why is it so unique for a diplomat to lecture before that group?

CHANG: I don't know. Possibly because they don't like diplomats.

CONTE: Well, how do you define diplomat? Does it just mean a tactful person?

CHANG: I think it goes a little deeper than tact. I can best illustrate the difference between tact and diplomacy by quoting a maxim laid down by an ancient Chinese scholar. It goes something like this. Should one, by chance, invade the privacy of a lady's bath while she is bathing—

MERE: Uh-huh.

CHANG: He displays great tact by saying "Pardon me, madam."

CONTE: And the diplomat?

CHANG: He says, "Pardon me, SIR."

CONTE: Seems to me like one of our American scholars, Joe Miller, once said the same thing.

CHANG: It's very possible—that gag's been kicked around a good deal.

MERE:	He sure knows a lot of slang for a foreign minister.
CHANG:	I can explain that, Mr. Willson. You see, I'm very fond of radio programs—and comedians—and I never miss this program at all.
CONTE:	Then you're acquainted with the personality of our Frank Morgan?
CHANG:	He fascinates me. I expect Mr. Morgan to dash on the stage here at any moment, throw a bundle of laundry at me and say, "Have this ready by Friday."
MORGAN:	(COMING ON) That's right - but I want the collars starched!
CONTE:	Frank!
	(APPLAUSE)
MORGAN:	My dear Dr. Chang! How wonderful to see you again! I trust both you and the lovely Mrs. Chang are enjoying good health?
CHANG:	Indeed we are, Frank. She constantly asks for you, and I'm so happy to see you looking so very fit!
MORGAN:	Splendid! Will you both take dinner with me this evening, my dear friend?
CHANG:	Delighted! Sevenish?
MORGAN:	Er—eightish. Don't be latish.
CONTE:	Er—excuse me. You two know each other?
MORGAN:	Know each other! Jockey, am I in the habit of embracing strangers?
CONTE:	Well, you—
MORGAN:	I mean male strangers!
CONTE:	Oh.
MORGAN:	As representatives in Europe of our respective nations it was my good fortune to cross the path of the learned doctor many —-
CONTE:	Wait a minute! What's this about representing a nation?
MORGAN:	Dear doctor, please enlighten this crass occidental.
CHANG:	You wish me to inform him about your European activities, Frank?
MORGAN:	Just my—shall we say—political activities. Tell him how and where we met.
CHANG:	Very well. It was in Monte Carlo at the chemin-de-fer table—
MORGAN:	(RAPIDLY) Er—you see fellows, that's a sort of a conference table. Chemin-de-fer. French, of course.

CONTE:	Of course.
MORGAN:	Of course. Continue, doctor.
CHANG:	You were a wonderful croupier, Frank.
MORGAN:	Croupier—that's Latin for negotiator. You needn't tell them any more, doctor. I'm sure Jockey's convinced that I was an ambassador.
CONTE:	Ambassador!
MORGAN:	Envoy Extraordinary and Minister Plenipotentiary to the Principality of Monaco, ruled for centuries by the ancient house of Maxwell. (I think I got the wrong grind there.)
CONTE:	Never mind the grind, drip.
MORGAN:	Oh, dripgrind.
CONTE:	Since when does America send an ambassador to a gambling joint?
MORGAN:	Well, my embassy was not actually in Monaco—although it's true most of my official business was conducted in the Casino. I've always been a firm believer in the old adage, women and song.
CONTE:	What about wine?
MORGAN:	Well, I was a minister without port, Folio. But the place was seething with spies and I even had to pose as a black-jack dealer to hoodwink them. Isn't that true, doctor?
CHANG:	I did see you dealing at the black-jack table.
MORGAN:	There!
CHANG:	But I could never understand why you took over the washroom concession.
MORGAN:	The tips were better. Ah—those were dangerous days and nights! But I didn't remain in Monaco very long. An unfortunate incident occurred which caused my transfer to a post in the romantic swampland of Siberia.
CHANG:	A very coveted assignment. (BEAMS AT HIM)
MORGAN:	Dear Dr. Chang.
CONTE:	What was the incident that washed you up in Monaco, Frank?
MORGAN:	A chivalrous intention on my part was misinterpreted. It was the evening of my presentation at court and the great hall was jammed with royalty from all the capitals of Europe. Beautiful women thronged around me—but my heart was beating only for the exotic Princesse de la Mink.

CHANG: A truly glamorous lady. (REMINISCES) Princesse de la Mink. Ah, yes.

MORGAN: (HAPPY) Oh, this fellow's worth his weight in gold as a straight man.

CONTE: Okay! What about the Princesse?

MORGAN: I had never seen her in person before, but I knew I would be able to identify her by the family motto inscribed on her coronet—just one Latin word—Levito.

CONTE: Levito—what's that?

MORGAN: I raise.

CONTE: I call—what have you got?

MORGAN: Three tens.

CONTE: No good—straight flush.

MORGAN: I haven't won a pot all ni—what are we talking about!

CHANG: Mr. Conte, I wish you'd refrain from interrupting Frank's extremely interesting story. Pray, continue, Frank.

MORGAN: Well! If he'd throw in a jeepers—we could do away with Meredith, too!

MERE: (OFF) Looks like I've been done away with for two weeks now.

MORGAN: Have no fears, son—I'm trying to put that condition on a permanent basis.

MERE: (GLOWING) And I thought you were trying to knife me! What a pal he is! I feel like a heel for ever suspect—

MORGAN: Go away.

MERE: Sure. Guy's got a heart of gold.

MORGAN: Oh dear.

CONTE: Did you find the Princesse, Frank?

MORGAN: I looked high and low for her, combing every inch of the palace. I finally came across her at the bar. She'd been standing there for over two hours.

CHANG: You mean you didn't go near the bar for two hours?

MORGAN: Hmm. I think this story needs a little revision. But when a man is hopelessly in love he'll suffer unbearable torture to be near the thing he loves most.

CONTE: The bar.

MORGAN: Exactly. NO! I bowed low before the regal lady, and asked if I might have the pleasure of the next polka. As we danced I whispered pretty compliments to her, and remarked how stunning she looked in her court gown.

CHANG: Yes?

MORGAN: Gaining confidence, I kissed her lightly on the cheek and breathed, "Countess, you look ravishing in that dress—and the bustle is so becoming." That same night I was transferred to Siberia.

CONTE: Why?

MORGAN: She wasn't wearing any bustle. It was an awful lot to leave behind, and I arrived in Siberia in a very depressed state. But my adventures were just to begin.

CONTE: Dr. Chang, are you familiar with the incident that Frank just told?

CHANG: I knew he was expelled from France, but I didn't know why.

MORGAN: As one diplomat to another, doctor—does it really matter?

CHANG: Not in the slightest.

MORGAN: Thank you. Upon opening the legation in Siberia I was amazed to learn that three of my attaches were in the employ of a foreign government, and a set of important documents had disappeared.

CONTE: I've been waiting for this.

MORGAN: I shadowed the three traitors day and night and found they were in contact with a group of foreign agents who'd made their headquarters in the rear of a bowling alley.

CHANG: Isn't a bowling alley rather a noisy place for spies?

MORGAN: It was so quiet you could hear a pin drop. (That wasn't even a spare!) I was anxious to hear their conversation, and I knew they'd be suspicious of dictaphones, so I constructed, with great ingenuity, a dictaphone that looked exactly like a radio.

CONTE: How'd you get it in their room?

MORGAN: I disguised myself as a bellboy and presented the radio to the spies along with a pitcher of ice-water.

CHANG: Ingenious!

MORGAN: Yes. I rushed pell-mell to a broom-closet down the corridor, where I'd concealed the receiver, and clapped the earphones to my head. Imagine my horror when I suddenly heard the chambermaid approaching!

CONTE:	What did you do?
MORGAN:	I stood on my head and disguised myself as a mop. Fortunately, she chose the mop next to me, who later turned out to be a spy from another country. I remained immobile, with the earphones still glued to my ears.
CHANG:	Did you pick anything up?
MORGAN:	Just the chambermaid's sister who happened to—oh! You mean information! Yes. Suddenly words began to filter through—somebody said Royal Canadians.
CONTE:	They were plotting the destruction of a regiment!
MORGAN:	No - Guy Lombardo played "Blues in the Night." I'd evidently gone astray while hooking up the dictaphone. Well, I won't bore you with the rest of the details—but I never found the documents.
CHANG:	What a pity!
CONTE:	Dr. Chang—do you actually believe there's an atom of truth in that whole fantastic story?
CHANG:	I most certainly do! And I can prove it!
MORGAN:	You can?
CHANG:	Positively. I was the mop standing next to you in the broom closet.
MORGAN:	Listen, I didn't mind when you did straight like Jockey, or grabbed off Meredith's lines—but when you try to take my job I'm thru! So long, fellows—I never could stand exaggeration!
	(MUSIC...APPLAUSE)
	MIDDLE COMMERCIAL
CONTE:	Well, Meredith—Sunday is Easter. Trees and bushes are bursting into bloom. You know—"In the Spring a young man's fancy" and all that, makes me feel romantic.
MERE:	Me, too, John. And it's really wonderful how Nature waits until Spring to shuck her old faded grays and sprout her new *rich* greens.
CONTE:	And how summer brings vegetation its *full body* of foliage.
MERE:	Including weeds and poison ivy! But Autumn adds deep red, soft yellow, golden brown...the months of *mellowness*.
CONTE:	While winter's robust *vigor* ends the cycle of the seasons...each playing its part in our full enjoyment of every passing year.
MERE:	Gee...ain't Nature grand?

WILCOX:	That it is, Meredith…that it is. And thank you both for the illustration.
CONTE:	Illustration of *what*, Harlow?

(START COMMERCIAL TIME HERE…188 WORDS, 1 MINUTE, 5 SECONDS)

WILCOX:	Why, Maxwell House Coffee! I mean—the characteristics you and Meredith just gave to the four *seasons* also apply to those extra-flavor, highland-grown *coffees* in the Maxwell House *blend*.
MERE:	They *do*? Well, what do you know?
WILCOX:	Sure. It's like this. In blending Maxwell House Coffee, we match the *richness* of Spring with premium Medelline…the *full body* of summer with prime Bucaramangas…the *mellowness* of autumn with choice Manizales…the *vigorous* tang of winter with Central and South Americans.
CONTE:	And each of these rare coffees contributes its own *special* quality to the fragrance and flavor of the superb Maxwell House blend…a blend far more *delicious* today than it was more than half a century ago…when created for Colonel Overton's celebrated old Maxwell House in Nashville, Tennessee.
WILCOX:	But remember…while those premium coffees command a premium price, Maxwell House costs *you* only a *fraction* of a penny more per cup than the cheapest coffees sold!
	So friends…if you haven't tried Maxwell House *lately*, why not enjoy it tomorrow? You'll find that now, more than ever…Maxwell House Coffee *is*…Good to the last drop!
CONTE:	Thank you—and thank you, Meredith. Say, I wonder why I haven't heard from daddy.
MEREDITH:	Why don't you give him a ring?
CONTE:	I'll do that…(DIALS)…You know, yesterday was April Fools day, and Snooks might have caused some trouble.
MERE:	Snooks? Go on—she never causes any trouble.
BRICE:	(FILTER) Hello.
CONTE:	Hello. Is that you, Snooks?
BRICE:	Hello.
CONTE:	Hello. This is John Conte.
BRICE:	Hello.

CONTE:	Hello! Who is this?	
BRICE:	This is the operator. Five cents please.	
CONTE:	Snooks! It is you, isn't it?	
BRICE:	No, this is my father. Wanna play poker?	
CONTE:	Where's your daddy?	
BRICE:	He jumped out the window, and a big eagle grabbed him by the—	
FATHER:	(FILTER) Give me that phone! Hello, John.	
CONTE:	Hello.	
FATHER:	I'll see you soon. I have to rush out as soon as I put Snooks to bed and buy a suit. Goodbye.	
CONTE:	Goodbye. (HANGS UP) I'll lay nine to five he never gets out.	

(SNOOKS PLAY-ON)

FATHER:	Snooks, I don't want you to answer the phone any more!
BRICE:	Why?
FATHER:	Because you say a lot of crazy things and confuse people. Why did you tell John I jumped out of the window?
BRICE:	He didn't believe me, daddy.
FATHER:	Then why did you say it?
BRICE:	'Cause I always say it.
FATHER:	You always tell him I just jumped out of the window?
BRICE:	Uh-huh.
FATHER:	What for?
BRICE:	I dunno.
FATHER:	Suppose I do jump out of the window one day, and you tell him that—he won't believe you, will he?
BRICE:	No.
FATHER:	Then what'll you do?
BRICE:	What will *you* do?
FATHER:	Snooks, have you ever heard the story of the little boy who cried wolf?
BRICE:	No. Tell it to me.
FATHER:	Well, I stuck my neck out that time. I'll tell it to you tomorrow. I'm in a hurry to get to the clothing store.

BRICE:	Why?
FATHER:	I'm going to be fitted for an Easter suit.
BRICE:	When is Easter, daddy?
FATHER:	Sunday. It's a little later than usual this year.
BRICE:	Why?
FATHER:	I don't know. It just happens to fall on the 5th. You see, Easter Sunday is governed by the date of the Paschal full moon. If the Paschal full moon falls on a Sunday then the following Sunday is Easter.
BRICE:	Is the moon gonna fall?
FATHER:	The moon is not going to fall. At least, according to the scientists, there's no danger of the moon falling for the next seventy million years.
BRICE:	Will it fall on the people?
FATHER:	I suppose so.
BRICE:	Waaahhhh!
FATHER:	What are you crying about? It won't happen for at least seventy million years.
BRICE:	Oh. I thought you said seven million.
FATHER:	Well, now you don't have to worry any more. Goodnight.
BRICE:	Goodnight…Daddy?
FATHER:	Yes?
BRICE:	Why does the moon make it Easter?
FATHER:	Well, the Paschal full moon is the fourteenth day of the lunar month reckoned according to an old ecclesiastical computation and not the real or astronomical full moon.
BRICE:	You know everything, don't you, daddy?
FATHER:	Just about. Any more questions?
BRICE:	Uh-huh. Why does Easter fall on Sunday?
FATHER:	I just told you!
BRICE:	Tell me again.
FATHER:	What for?
BRICE:	I like to see your neck get red.

FATHER:	Well, I won't say it again. Easter falls on April 5th this year because it was pushed back.
BRICE:	Who pushed it?
FATHER:	Nobody pushed it!
BRICE:	Then how did it fall?
FATHER:	Listen! Easter Sunday has no definite set date and it may fall any time between March 22nd and April 25th. This year it happens to fall on April 5th!
BRICE:	Why?
FATHER:	Because it does!
BRICE:	Well, who tells the bunnies when it's Easter?
FATHER:	They don't have to be told!
BRICE:	Then how do they know when to lay the eggs?
FATHER:	Bunnies don't lay eggs!
BRICE:	Why?
FATHER:	How do I know!
BRICE:	Chickens lay eggs.
FATHER:	I can't help it!
BRICE:	Why?
FATHER:	Snooks—I'll explain it to you in the morning. The tailor's waiting to measure me for my suit.
BRICE:	I wanna go with you.
FATHER:	Snooks!
BRICE:	I wanna go with you!
FATHER:	You can't go with me! Can't I buy a suit of clothes without having you tag along?
BRICE:	Mummy's going, ain't she?
FATHER:	Not this time she isn't! I'm going to wear what *I* like for once in my life. I'm sick of these bell-bottom pants!
BRICE:	Your coat is nice, daddy.
FATHER:	Nice! You call this pinchback, one-button misfit nice?
BRICE:	I like the way it zips up in the back.

FATHER:	You and your mummy! I'll show you style—wait till I come home with my new suit. I'm getting a spring coat, too.
BRICE:	With springs in it?
FATHER:	No - not with springs in it! A nice conservative model with padded shoulders and a flared waistline—just a few pleats on the hem.
BRICE:	Are you gonna get a hat with feathers in it again?
FATHER:	Don't be sarcastic. I'm buying this coat at Squires because they have a bargain sale. A thirty-five dollar coat marked down to nine seventy-five.
BRICE:	How do you know, daddy?
FATHER:	Because he advertised it that way. All his coats are down.
BRICE:	Are his pants down, too?
FATHER:	What's the matter with you?
BRICE:	I wanna go with you.
FATHER:	Now, Snooks—why would you want to go to the tailor's with me?
BRICE:	I wanna get an Easter suit.
FATHER:	You'll have a new dress—I promise you. Goodnight.
BRICE:	Goodnight, daddy…Daddy?
FATHER:	Oh, what do you want?
BRICE:	Who lays the Easter eggs?
FATHER:	I thought we'd settled that! Are you just trying to detain me so that mummy'll catch me before I leave?
BRICE:	Uh-huh.
FATHER:	Well, it won't help!
BRICE:	Then tell me who lays the Easter eggs.
FATHER:	If I tell you will you let me go?
BRICE:	Maybe.
FATHER:	All right. Do you want the rabbit to lay the Easter eggs?
BRICE:	No.
FATHER:	Do you want the chicken to lay them?
BRICE:	No.
FATHER:	Well, who do you want to lay the eggs?

BRICE:	You.
FATHER:	Okay—I'll lay the Easter eggs. Satisfied?
BRICE:	No—lay one now.
FATHER:	I will not! Snooks—please let me get out of the house. You want me to look nice, don't you?
BRICE:	Yes, daddy.
FATHER:	Fine! And I'll buy you a new dress—and when I put on my new suit and coat we'll be the hit of the Easter parade.
BRICE:	Will you buy me a rabbit, too?
FATHER:	A live rabbit?
BRICE:	Yeah—a live rabbit.
FATHER:	Oh, no. No rabbits in this house. I'll buy you a nice chocolate rabbit though.
BRICE:	I don't want no chocolate rabbit.
FATHER:	You don't want a big chocolate one that you can eat?
BRICE:	No—I wanna eat a live one.
FATHER:	You little cannibal! All right—I'll buy you a live rabbit.
BRICE:	A white rabbit?
FATHER:	Yes—a white rabbit!
BRICE:	I don't like white rabbits.
FATHER:	Well, what kind do you want?
BRICE:	I want a blue rabbit with purple legs and a green tail.
FATHER:	You're insane! Either you take a white rabbit or you get nothing.
BRICE:	I'll take it, daddy.
FATHER:	And remember—you'll have to care for it yourself. No rough handling. You'll treat it just like a baby.
BRICE:	Like a baby?
FATHER:	Yes. You'll handle the rabbit exactly the way mother handles Robespierre.
BRICE:	Will I have to change his—
FATHER:	Yes! You'll have to change his water every day.
BRICE:	That ain't what I was—

FATHER:	I don't care what you were going to say! And I'm not going to waste another second here! Goodnight!
BRICE:	Goodnight, daddy…Daddy?
FATHER:	(SOBS) Oh, what is it now!
BRICE:	You ain't really gonna buy me a rabbit, are you?
FATHER:	Well—I'll think about it.
BRICE:	When?
FATHER:	Tonight. If you get right into bed, turn out the light, say your prayers, and ask the angels to make you a good girl—maybe I'll bring a rabbit home with me.
BRICE:	Awight, daddy.
FATHER:	Good…Hurry now…Under the covers…Out with the light…Now, say your prayers.
BRICE:	(MUMBLES A LOT OF DOUBLETALK)
FATHER:	What are you mumbling?
BRICE:	That's my prayers.
FATHER:	I can't understand a word you're saying.
BRICE:	I ain't talking to you—I'm talking to the angels.
FATHER:	Well, they can't understand you, either. Speak up.
BRICE:	Awight…Dear angels, please make my daddy a good boy so he'll bring home a rabbit tonight. Signing off.
FATHER:	Snooks! That's no way to talk to the angels!
BRICE:	They like it, daddy.
FATHER:	How do you know?
BRICE:	I'll show you…You like it, don't you, angels? (DIFFERENT VOICE) That's okay with us, Snooks—you'll get your rabbit.
FATHER:	Ahhh—goodnight!
BRICE:	(LAUGHS) Goodnight, daddy.
	(MUSIC…APPLAUSE)
	CLOSING COMMERCIAL
MERE:	Oh, John!
CONTE:	Yes, Meredith!

MERE:	Here's a little thing I worked out to illustrate a point. Listen!
	(VIOLIN...FIRST 5 NOTES OF THEME, VERY SOUR)
	That was a *trumpet* tooter trying to play the violin. Now...
	(PIANO...SAME 5 NOTES, ALSO SOUR)
	A *violinist* taking a slap at the ivories. Next...
	(TRUMPET...SAME 5 NOTES, EVEN WORSE)
	And the *pianist* attempting to trumpet. Get the idea, John?
CONTE:	Perfectly...that a musician had better stick to his *own instrument!*
	START COMMERCIAL TIME HERE...193 WORDS...1 MINUTE, 6 SECONDS
MERE:	Sure. And I hope the ladies will understand that the same idea applies to making coffee...better stick to the right *grind* for the brewing *method* they use.
WILCOX:	*Exactly* why Maxwell House Coffee comes already precisely ground *three* ways...for Drip, Regular, or Glass-Maker methods. The right grind makes better coffee...and more *economically*, too. Besides that, Maxwell House is more convenient to buy...no *waiting* for *store* grinding!
CONTE:	And today, every pound—however ground—gives you *more* for your money in other ways. For instance, there's more flavor in the Maxwell House *blend*.
WILCOX:	Because it's *extra* rich in extra-flavor, highland-grown coffees!
CONTE:	More flavor in the *cup*.
WILCOX:	Because our special "Radiant Roast" process is designed to develop the *full* flavor of every bean!
CONTE:	More *freshness*, as well.
WILCOX:	In fact, Maxwell House is *roaster*-fresh...vacuum-sealed in the new Duraglas jar and the familiar blue can to keep air *out* and flavor *in!* And for more *economy*...to save money and shopping trips, too...there's the thrifty *two-pound* size.
	So if you ladies *really* want *more* for your coffee money today...just you ask for *Maxwell House* Coffee...tomorrow!
MORGAN:	This is the story of the farmer in the dell. Who had a plough, and a horse and cow, and a little goose as well.
BRICE:	Just a goose?

MORGAN: Yes, a goose—but not an ordinary goose which brings us to the breakfast food this webfoot did produce.

One day while making his customary round, he looked into the goose's nest and what do you think he found?

BRICE: A banana!

MORGAN: No.

BRICE: Polliwog!

MORGAN: No.

BRICE: Well, what did he find?

MORGAN: An egg!

BRICE: Just an egg?

MORGAN: Yes, an egg—but not an ordinary egg. Categorically speaking, this egg was up a peg. It brightly shone—but hard as stone. In fact he couldn't bust it—

BRICE: Uncle Frank!

MORGAN: (WITH A SIGH) What now?

BRICE: I wanna ask you something.

MORGAN: Is it important?

BRICE: Yeah—very important.

MORGAN: All right—what is it?

BRICE: Does a goose lay an egg 'cause it wants to or must it?

MORGAN: Who cares!

BRICE: The goose.

MORGAN: Will you please let me finish?

BRICE: All right.

MORGAN: Lo and behold, the egg was gold—a nugget at its best, which ev'ry day the goose did lay like clockwork in her nest. Because of which he soon grew rich. But soon the silly dunce began to dream of some mad scheme to get all the gold at once.

Oh, greed, tis said, will turn one's head—and make the sage unsound. So he killed the goose and opened it,

And what do you think he found?

BRICE:	Chopped chicken liver?
MORGAN:	No.
BRICE:	Gooseberries.
MORGAN:	No.
BRICE:	Well, what did he find?
MORGAN:	Nothing.
BRICE:	Waaaahhhh!
MORGAN:	What are you crying for?
BRICE:	I don't like it.
MORGAN:	Neither did the farmer.
BOTH:	There's a moral to this fable. Better paste it on the label. Of your bonnet. Mark it well of you I beg. January to December One and all you should remember— "Do not kill the goose that lays the golden egg".

(APPLAUSE)

THEME...FADING FOR

CONTE:	Which about takes us to the bottom of the page, ladies and gentlemen, but we'll be back again next Thursday evening at Maxwell House Coffee Time...Fanny Brice as Baby Snooks, Frank Morgan, who appears with us thru the courtesy of Metro-Goldwyn-Mayer, Hanley Stafford Meredith Willson and his orchestra, and Harlow Wilcox.
	Maxwell House Coffee Time is written by Phil Rapp.
	Until next Thursday then, this is John Conte saying goodnight and good luck from the makers of Maxwell House...the coffee that is always...good to the last drop!

HITCH HIKE

ANNOUNCER:	(TO BE READ IN THIRTY SECONDS EXACTLY) N-U-C-O-A...that spells NUCOA...the delicious spread for bread that helps balance the budget and the diet, too! Yes, indeed...every pound of NUCOA...the modern mar-jer-in...contains nine thousand units of protective Vitamin A...and it's nourishing,

good for all the family! What's more, NUCOA gives all your cooking—all your baking the rich, homey flavor that only a spread for bread *can* give. And...best of all, it's *thrifty*! You *save* money...with delicious, wholesome NUCOA!

"SCREEN GUILD SHOW"
SUNDAY, MARCH 19, 1939
4:30 - 5:00 P.M.

ORCHESTRA: (THEME...FADES FOR)

CONTE: Welcome, everybody. Tonight your neighborhood Good Gulf Dealer joins the Gulf Oil Companies in presenting another program in this series of revues, musical comedies and dramatic shows—all the varied entertainment forms of Hollywood. So, welcome all of you to the motion picture stars' own program—welcome to the "Gulf Screen Guild Show!"

MUSIC: (UP...HOLD...FADE)

CONTE: With...Fanny Brice.

MUSIC: (BUILD)

CONTE: Bob Hope.

MUSIC: (BUILD)

CONTE: Martha Raye.

MUSIC: (BUILD)

CONTE: Hanley Stafford.

MUSIC: (BUILD)

CONTE: OSCAR BRADLEY...

MUSIC: (BUILD)

CONTE: And Hollywood's favorite master of ceremonies...George Murphy!

(APPLAUSE)

MUSIC: (FADES BEHIND)

MURPHY: Good evening, ladies and gentlemen...and welcome to another of the motion picture stars' own programs...THE "GULF SCREEN GUILD SHOW"...Each week a different type of entertainment...presenting a different cast of stars...and all of them written, directed and acted by the greatest names in the motion picture industry...for the benefit of the Motion Picture Relief Fund. Last week it was a comedy...next week a drama, starring Leslie Howard, _____, and Virginia Weidler...and tonight, it's a revue starring Fanny Brice, Bob Hope, Martha Raye and Hanley Stafford...directed by Norman Taurog and written by Phil Rapp...under the musical direction of Oscar Bradley.

On with the show! And our first Screen Guild Star for tonight...Martha Raye!

(APPLAUSE)

MURPHY: (WITH GUSTO) Hello, Martha!!

RAYE: (SWANKY) How do you do, Mister Murphy...Charmed to be here, I'm sure.

MURPHY: Wait a minute, Martha...that doesn't sound like you. Haven't you changed since the last time I saw you?

RAYE: Oh, rawther...you see, I'm a married woman now and that makes one sort of Comment Ca Va, nes pass?

MURPHY: Martha, you certainly have changed.

RAYE: Exactly...Ask me a question, and I'll show you how I used to be.

MURPHY: All right. May I call on you tonight, Martha?

RAYE: Oh boy!!...You said it, kid, yahoo!!...(SWEETLY) That's how I used to be...Rahlly. Now ask me that same question today.

MURPHY: All right. May I call on you tonight, Martha?

RAYE: Pray do!...You see, I'm a lady.

MURPHY: Of course you're a lady.

RAYE: Yes, I'm a perfect lady...(YELLS) And I'll rassle anybody who sez I ain't!!

MURPHY: All right, all right...nobody denies it. To make you feel at home I'll introduce you to a perfect little gentleman...Oh, Oscar...where are you, Oscar?

BRADLEY: (COMING IN) Here I am, Mr. Murphy. I'm coming.

RAYE: Wait...don't tell me...give me three guesses.

MURPHY:	This is Oscar Bradley, our orchestra leader. Where were you, Oscar—you were supposed to be here by my side?
BRADLEY:	I was, but when Miss Raye yelled she blew me into the balcony.
RAYE:	It's a lucky thing I didn't really yell or you'd be hitch-hiking back from Pasadena.
MURPHY:	Well, come on, Oscar…I'll nail you down to the podium so you won't blow away while Martha Raye sings "Taint Necessarily So."

ORCHESTRA AND MARTHA RAYE: – "TAINT NECESSARILY SO"

MURPHY:	Now a word from John Conte.

(COMMERCIAL "A")

CONTE:	Ladies and gentlemen…they say that seeing is believing. Well, tonight I'd like to tell you about a time when HEARING is believing…and that's when you *hear* the way Gulf No-Nox Ethyl gasoline quiets down your car and ENDS MOTOR KNOCKS. You've heard motor knocks in your car often enough—when you're driving up a steep hill…or when you accelerate suddenly on the level. Well—just try a tankful of Gulf No-Nox…drive up the same steep hill or accelerate in the same way…and LISTEN…With No-Nox in your tank you don't hear the same annoying pinging sound at all. Instead…your motor gives you quieter, smoother performance almost immediately—and in the long run you probably save money on your upkeep expenses, too. So won't you drive in tomorrow at the sign of the Gulf Orange Disc and try just one tankful of Gulf No-Nox gasoline!

(COMMERCIAL TAG)

RAYE:	Oh, George—
MURPHY:	What is it, Martha?
RAYE:	I never did get it straight—just who is going to be on tonight?
MURPHY:	Well, let's see—there's Bob Hope.
RAYE:	Oh, that's good.
MURPHY:	And you—
RAYE:	Oh, that's marvellous.
MURPHY:	And then there's Fannie Brice—Baby Snooks—
RAYE:	You know—they're two of my favorite comedians.…

MURPHY:	Now, wait a minute—Fannie Brice *is* Baby Snooks, and Hanley Stafford is her daddy.
RAYE:	Really?...I've got to see that...Where is she?...Where's Baby Snooks?
MURPHY:	Well, she couldn't make it tonight, Martha, because her daddy is sick. But we've rigged up special wires to her home, where her daddy is sick in bed with a nervous disorder. The doctor has just finished his examination. Our engineer will make a connection, and we'll listen.
SOUND:	CLICK OF SWITCH
FATHER:	Well, doctor—do you think I'll be all right?
DOCTOR:	Oh yes. The rash has almost disappeared. I'd advise you to stay in bed a few more days, though.
FATHER:	Well, I was a little worried about the work piling up at the office so I had them send this dictaphone out. Is it all right if I dictate a few letters?
DOCTOR:	I don't think that'll hurt. But stay as quiet as possible. Don't give that rash a chance to break out again.
FATHER:	I'll be careful, doctor.
DOCTOR:	Above all—no excitement of any kind, remember!
FATHER:	Okay, doctor. No excitement.
DOCTOR:	Well, I have to be running along now...Goodbye.
FATHER:	Goodbye—and thanks...(DOOR SLAM)...Hmmm, now let's see this mail...Guess I'd better answer this one first...Where's that dictaphone switch?...Oh, here...(CLEARS THROAT) Gentlemen...yours of the fifteenth instant received and contents noted...In reply, would say—
BRICE:	Hello, Daddy.
FATHER:	Snooks! I've asked you not to disturb me this morning—I'm busy.
BRICE:	Was the doctor here, Daddy?
FATHER:	Yes, he just left. Now run along.
BRICE:	Awight.
FATHER:	(CLEARS THROAT) Gentlemen...yours of the fifteenth instant received and contents—
BRICE:	Daddy.

FATHER:	Are you still here?
BRICE:	Did the doctor bring his little black bag?
FATHER:	Yes.
BRICE:	Have I been a good girl—Daddy?
FATHER:	Yes.
BRICE:	Well, ain't you gonna let me see the baby?
FATHER:	There isn't any baby! Now please leave me alone—I'm supposed to have absolute quiet!
BRICE:	I wanna stay here.
FATHER:	Snooks, the doctor said if I get excited I'll break out in a rash again! Now go away and let me get these letters off.
BRICE:	Awight, Daddy.
FATHER:	(CLEARS THROAT) Gentlemen…yours of the fifteenth instant received—
BRICE:	Daddy?
FATHER:	What do you want?
BRICE:	Who you talking to?
FATHER:	I'm not talking to anybody. That is, I'm talking to my secretary but she's not here.
BRICE:	Do you feel all right, Daddy?
FATHER:	Yes—I feel fine! And when I don't feel all right I'll take my medicine…leave me alone!…(CLEARS THROAT)… Gentlemen…Yours of the fifteenth—
BRICE:	Are you talking on the telephone?
FATHER:	No—this is a dictaphone. It's a dictating machine that plays records.
BRICE:	I don't hear no music.
FATHER:	It doesn't play music.
BRICE:	Then what's it for?
FATHER:	It's a machine that takes letters.
BRICE:	Like the mailman.
FATHER:	No!
BRICE:	Then where does it take them?

FATHER:	(SHOUTS) NOWHERE!…(VERY QUIETLY)…I mean, nowhere.
BRICE:	Can I see the letters, Daddy?
FATHER:	No—they're on this record.
BRICE:	What record?
FATHER:	This big black cylindrical thing. The letter is recorded on it.
BRICE:	How you gonna get it in an envelope?
FATHER:	It doesn't have to go in an envelope!
BRICE:	Then how can you mail it?
FATHER:	I'm not going to mail it! (SHOUTS) Will you please leave this room and let me work!
BRICE:	(LAUGHS) Oooooooooooh—lookit!
FATHER:	Look at what?
BRICE:	There's a strawberry on your face!
FATHER:	(ALMOST IN A WHISPER)…Gentlemen…yours of the fifteenth instant received and contents …
BRICE:	(IN THE SAME TONE) Daddy!
FATHER:	Oh, what's the use! Now what do you want?
BRICE:	There's another strawberry!
FATHER:	I know it, Snooks. You made me get excited and the rash is coming back.
BRICE:	Is that what it is?
FATHER:	Yes.
BRICE:	How'd you get it?
FATHER:	I ate something that didn't agree with me. So it comes out on my face.
BRICE:	Did you eat strawberries?
FATHER:	No—I ate fish.
BRICE:	You eat fish and a strawberry comes on your face?
FATHER:	Yes.
BRICE:	If you eat strawberries, will a fish come on your face?
FATHER:	No!
BRICE:	Why?

FATHER:	Because I'm not sensitive to strawberries—only to fish!
BRICE:	Ohhhhh…Daddy?
FATHER:	What is it?
BRICE:	Do fish eat strawberries?
FATHER:	How do I know? Leave me alone with the fish and strawberries—I have to work!
BRICE:	On the machine?
FATHER:	(SHOUTS) Yes…Gentlemen…Received your strawberry of the fifteenth fish and—ohhhhh! What am I saying?
BRICE:	You better take some medicine, Daddy.
FATHER:	(HOARSELY) I don't need any medicine—I'm all right. I'm calm—I'm not excited! I think I've got a fever.
BRICE:	What you putting in your mouth, Daddy?
FATHER:	I'm going to take my temperature.
BRICE:	With a cigar?
FATHER:	Ohhhh, am I sick. I don't know what I'm doing—where's the thermometer?
BRICE:	Here, Daddy.
FATHER:	Ohhhh!…Mmmmmmmmmm.
BRICE:	Does it taste good?
FATHER:	Mmmmmmm…mmmm…(GRUNTS)
BRICE:	Can't you talk with that thing in your mouth?
FATHER:	(MAKES UNINTELLIGIBLE NOISES) Mmmmmmm…mmm…
BRICE:	Ohhhh…Daddy?
FATHER:	Mmmmmmmmmmm?
BRICE:	I'm gonna say the letter for you in the machine.
FATHER:	(ALARMED) Mmmmmmmm…Mmmmmmmmmmmm.
BRICE:	Dear Uncle Louie…
FATHER:	(MOANS) Mmmmmmmmmm…mmmmmmmmm.
BRICE:	My daddy is very funny—he sucks on a glass lollipop and he can make strawberries come on his face whenever he wants to…Ummmmm.

FATHER:	Mmmmmmmmm…(SHOUTS) STOP PULLING ON THAT DICTAPHONE! SNOOKS—YOU'RE GOING TO…(TERRIFIC CRASH)…Ohhhh!
BRICE:	I think I better go out and play.
FATHER:	(MOANS) Look what you've done…the machine is wrecked… it'll cost me a hundred dollars…Ohhh—I'm sick…(SUDDENLY) Where's the thermometer?
BRICE:	You swallowed it, Daddy.
FATHER:	Ohhh! Good heavens! Call the doctor—I'm dying!…wait a minute, here's the thermometer—it fell on the bed…Oh, thank Heaven.
BRICE:	You feel better, Daddy?
FATHER:	(HOARSELY) Yes—yes.
BRICE:	There ain't no more strawberries on your face, Daddy.
FATHER:	(HOPEFULLY) No? Really?
BRICE:	No—now they look like tomatoes.
FATHER:	Oh…quick—get my medicine—that powder. Get a glass of water.
BRICE:	Shall I put the powder in the glass, Daddy?
FATHER:	Yes—not too much! Just enough to cover a dime…I'm dying.
BRICE:	Wait—I'll get a dime from my bank.
FATHER:	(GROANING) Oh…that dictaphone…a hundred dollars…I'll never get well…Snooks—hurry with the medicine!
BRICE:	Here, Daddy. Drink it down.
FATHER:	(DRINKS)…Hmmmmm…(SHRIEKS)…OHhhhhhhhhh! It burns… Snooks—How much powder did you put in this glass?
BRICE:	Huh?
FATHER:	I told you only to put in enough to cover a dime!
BRICE:	Well, I couldn't find a dime—so I used ten pennies!
	(APPLAUSE)
	(SNOOKS PLAY-OFF)
MUSIC:	(HITS AND FADES)
MURPHY:	Oscar Bradley might not be tall but he proves that he's a big man in things musically by swinging out with his own arrangement of "Could Be."

ORCHESTRA – "COULD BE"

MURPHY: Nice work, Oscar. That was "Could Be" as it should be.

BRADLEY: Thank you, George.

MURPHY: By the way, Oscar, who was that little feller I saw you with at the Biltmore last night?

BRADLEY: Oh, that was my big brother.

MURPHY: A fine big brother. I heard him complaining on the dance floor that people kept bumping him in the eye with their knees.

BRADLEY: Oh yes, he had an awful time. But it didn't bother me…I was too busy gazing into the eyes of that beautiful girl I was dancing with.

MURPHY: Say, she certainly was a beautiful girl. But, Oscar, why did you leave so early?

BRADLEY: Oh, my brother got tired dancing with me on his shoulders.

MURPHY: Don't worry about your brother, Oscar. You can always dance with Jane Withers…All you'll have to do is wear high heels…if she wears low ones.

HOPE: Did anyone mention heels?

MURPHY: Why, it's Bob Hope!

(APPLAUSE)

HOPE: Hello, George—Hello, Oscar.

BRADLEY: H'ya, Bob.

MURPHY: Say, I didn't know you two knew each other.

HOPE: Oh, sure I met him last night. I gave him a lift.

MURPHY: That was nice of you.

HOPE: I'll say it was. He wanted to kiss his girl good night and he couldn't find a ladder, so I gave him a lift. I didn't mind holding him up in my arms to kiss her, but he acted like a baby…Every time I put him down he cried…Honestly.

MURPHY: Well, if I were as short as Oscar, and in love with a tall girl, I wouldn't depend on anyone to lift me up…I'd make her wear a block and pulley for a necklace.

HOPE: Don't let it get you down, Oscar. I know how you feel. I went around with a tall girl once myself.

BRADLEY: Was she really tall, Bob?

HOPE:	Tall?...Oscar, she was so tall she had snow on her head six months out of the year...I wore out three pogo sticks trying to kiss her.
MURPHY:	Yep, you're the same old Bob...You know it's been a long time since I've seen you. Times have certainly changed.
HOPE:	I'll say times have changed. Remember?...You used to dance.
MURPHY:	Yeah, and you used to tell funny jokes.
	(AND INTO HOPE MONOLOGUE)
	(HOPE MONOLOGUE)
MUSIC:	(HITS AND FADES)
MURPHY:	One of the greatest love songs that ever came from the pen of George and Ira Gershwin becomes a Screen Guild highlight as Martha Raye sings "The Man I Love."
MUSIC:	"THE MAN I LOVE"
	(APPLAUSE)
MURPHY:	In just a minute, Fanny Brice, Bob Hope and Martha Raye will give you their version of a Gay Nineties melodrama, "Fifi, The Flame of Paris," but now let's hear a few words from John Conte—
	(COMMERCIAL "B")
CONTE:	With Spring officially only one day away...we'd like to extend a sincere invitation to all of you to let your neighborhood Good Gulf Dealer help you get ready for the new season. Of course, he can't come into your house and help with the cleaning...but he *can* help with the family car. For instance...now that we're having more warm days...it's wise to have him check the water in your radiator and in your storage battery. And...as a kind of a spring tonic...better have him fill your tank with that famous Gulf No-Nox Ethyl gasoline that we mentioned earlier this evening. Then you know that your car will give you top performance. Yes...for extra quality in BOTH products and service...stop at your independent neighborhood Good Gulf Dealer's. He takes a real *personal responsibility* for giving your car the *best possible care*. That's why it *pays* to make the Good Gulf Dealer *Your* Dealer.
MUSIC:	"TA RA RA BOOM DE AH"
MURPHY:	Tonight, ladies and gentlemen, the "Screen Guild Show" presents its version of that great epic of the nineties—"Fifi, the Flame of

	Paris," with Fanny Brice as Mademoiselle Fifi, Martha Raye as Charmaine, Bob Hope as Henri Toulouse, and I will play the part of Jack Pot—I hope nobody hits me...Johnnie, will you set the scene, please?
MUSIC:	"PARIS IN THE SPRING"
CONTE:	Paris...the Spring of 1894...Mademoiselle Fifi, the idol of Paris, is resting after the evening performance in her beautiful mansion atop an inaccessible mountain singing softly as Charmaine, her maid, (FADES) dresses her luxuriant hair.
MUSIC:	(OUT...FADE IN...PIANO CONTINUES ACCOMPANIMENT TO:)
BRICE:	(SINGS) I'm only a bird in a gilded cage, I'm Fifi the glamour girl. I once had a honey with plenty of cash Who called me his little pearl.
RAYE:	(SINGS) Then how come you lead a single life And still are upon the stage?
BRICE:	(SINGS) Someone else was preferred So I got the bird And she got the gilded cage.
SOUND:	HEAVY KNOCKING ON DOOR
BRICE:	Charmaine! Somebody is knocking at the door—It may be a man!
RAYE:	Whee!...I mean "oui," Mamselle. It must be that mystery man who has watched your performance every night for a month.
BRICE:	Do you think I should let him in?
RAYE:	Dear me, no...not in your home at this hour of the night.
BRICE:	It wouldn't be right, huh...Charmaine, is he handsome?
RAYE:	I don't know. I only saw him from the back.
BRICE:	Is he tall?
RAYE:	No, he's short.
BRICE:	Has he got blonde, wavy hair?
RAYE:	No, he's bald.
BRICE:	Hm, has he got maybe, a good physique?
RAYE:	Terrible.
BRICE:	Is he a man?

RAYE:	Yes.
BRICE:	Send him in!...Vive la France!
RAYE:	Vive la France!
BRICE:	Wait a...I'll let him in myself. You go into the other room.
RAYE:	All right...I'll comb your beautiful hair while I'm in there.
SOUND:	DOOR SLAMS...KNOCK ON DOOR
BRICE:	Come in.
SOUND:	DOOR OPENS
HOPE:	Oh, I beg your pardon...I must have knocked on the wrong door. I thought this was Schultz's butcher shop.
BRICE:	(ASIDE) How sly he is. (ALOUD) A very natural mistake. (ASIDE) Hm, he thought this was a butcher shop...What do I look like, lamb chops?
HOPE:	Pardon me, I'll be on my way. (ASIDE) I'll lay eight to five she calls me back. (ALOUD) Goodbye.
BRICE:	Goodbye. (ASIDE) I'll get him back here by dropping this wallet.
SOUND:	WALLET DROPS
BRICE:	Excuse me, did you drop this wallet?
HOPE:	Take your foot off it and I'll see.
BRICE:	Oh, excuse me. (ASIDE) If he reaches for it, I'll break his arm.
HOPE:	No, it's not mine...but off with this sham and pretence...Fifi, I know who you are, and I love you.
BRICE:	That's more like it! Won't you come in and sit down? I got plenty chairs in the room.
HOPE:	So I see...which one shall we sit on?
BRICE:	Come, let's sit in the Morris Chair near the Murphy bed.
HOPE:	Okay...Scram Morris...Get out of there, Murphy...Ah, Fifi,...I love you, my little French Pastry.
BRICE:	Yeh, yeh.
HOPE:	You're like a piece of strawberry shortcake.
BRICE:	Ah—ha!
HOPE:	You're as sweet as strawberry jam...Your lips are like strawberry tarts.

BRICE:	Ah, my love…come closer to me.
HOPE:	What…and get hives?
BRICE:	Don't worry…If I get you in my arms, you'll never break out…
HOPE:	Oh, that's music to my ears…Be mine and I'll make you the happiest girl in the world.
BRICE:	Could I try a kiss on approval?
HOPE:	Certainly, my sweet.
SOUND:	KISS
HOPE:	Ah…Pepsodent…Will you kiss me again?
BRICE:	What a question! (KISS) Take me, I'm a wilted pansy.
HOPE:	Will you fly with me?
BRICE:	Yes, I'll tell my maid to pack my things…Oh, Charmaine.
SOUND:	DOOR OPENS
RAYE:	Yes, Mademoiselle…I'm coming…YOU!!
HOPE:	Curses…my fiancée…Charmaine Dreep.
BRICE:	Aha! The plot thickens! You know him, Charmaine?
RAYE:	Know him? This man lured me from Jack, my sweetheart…promised to marry me…beat me…twisted my arm…took my money…kicked my dog…starved me…and left me waiting at the altar.
HOPE:	That's a lie! I never touched your dog.
RAYE:	How dare you talk to me like that?
HOPE:	Oh, twenty-three skiddoo, and I do mean skid—
BRICE:	Watch your language!
RAYE:	I am alone and helpless…Why do you insult me?
HOPE:	Because you're alone and helpless.
RAYE:	Yes, but remember—

My mother was a lady who always used her bean,
She warned me that you'd leave me ere the wedding ring turned green.
You've treated me so awful, you made it your career,
But you wouldn't dare insult me, sir, if Jack were only here.

(HOLDS LAST NOTE…OVER LAST NOTE BANGING ON DOOR…DOOR BURSTS OPEN)

MURPHY:	But I am here!
ORCHESTRA:	(CHEERS MADLY)
MURPHY:	Unhand her, you villain…that's the girl I love.
RAYE:	Hey! I'm over here.
MURPHY:	(VERY CASUALLY) Oh, hello Charmaine, what are you doing here? (TO HOPE) Take your hands off Fifi, the girl I love.
HOPE:	She's mine!
MURPHY:	No, she's mine!
RAYE:	Well, what about me?
HOPE:	Fifi's mine, you cur. And if you want her…you'll have to spill the blood of Henri Toulouse!
BRICE:	Vive la France…but look out for my new rug.
RAYE:	A fight—Oh boy! Break him in half. Tear him in two…In the la Bonza.
MURPHY:	No! There's only one way to settle this…we'll let the cards decide.
HOPE:	Okay…the cards. One game of pinochle. We'll play for Fifi's love…and on the side, ten cents a hundred.
BRICE:	What…Is that all you think of my honor?
HOPE:	All right, make it twenty cents a hundred.
BRICE:	I still refuse to let you play pinochle for my love…Let's play bridge…We can all make some money.
HOPE:	All right…I'll be Fifi's partner…do you play bridge, Fifi?
BRICE:	Like a duck.
HOPE:	Fine…Will you two hold your ears for a minute? I want to set the signals with my partner?
MURPHY:	All right…but no cheating.
HOPE:	Now listen…it's very simple…if I talk about my heart, you bid hearts. If I admire your ring, you bid diamonds. If I say I was digging in the garden, you bid spades. And if I mention the Elks, you bid clubs. Got it?
BRICE:	It's a cinch.
MURPHY:	Come on…the cards are all dealt.
RAYE:	Oh, what is to become of me? Both the men in my life in love with another woman…this is a fate worse than death.. one club.

HOPE: I pass.

MURPHY: One heart. What do you bid, Fifi?

BRICE: Er—let me see—

HOPE: What's that on your finger, Fifi?

BRICE: A mole.

HOPE: A mole? That's the first square cut mole I've ever seen. I was talking about your other finger...The one with the ring...It's beautiful.

BRICE: You like it? I won it in a raffle.

HOPE: Pay attention, Fifi...I mean the stone in the ring.

MURPHY: It's as big as an Elk's tooth.

BRICE: Aha! Elks!...Two clubs...

HOPE: No—No—

RAYE: I pass.

HOPE: Two spades.

MURPHY: Three hearts.

BRICE: Hm, it's my turn, huh?

HOPE: Here we go again...You know what I was doing yesterday, Fifi, I was digging in my garden.

BRICE: Digging in your garden?

HOPE: Yes.

BRICE: Hm, that's good exercise, ain't it?

HOPE: Yes, you can work up a lot of steam if you have the tools to dig with...I have three of them.

BRICE: I get it...I get it...Three steamshovels.

HOPE: Fifi, move your head over here, so I can get my lips close to your ear.

BRICE: You want to whisper something?

HOPE: No, I want to use it for a beanshooter...Not steamshovels...Digging in my garden...Remember, spades...

MURPHY: Just a minute, Henri...I'm wise to you...You're cheating...Take that...

SOUND: TWO SHOTS

RAYE:	Police! Help! He killed Henri!
BRICE:	He's dead…Oh well, he had a rotten hand anyway.
MURPHY:	Oh, I'm a murderer, and it's all your fault, Fifi.
BRICE:	My fault?
MURPHY:	Yes. (SINGS "CURSE OF AN ACHING HEART")
	You made me what I am today. I hope you're satisfied. To please your whim, I shot at him, till he curled up and died. I'll prob'ly get what I deserve. But now that we must part, I can't help but feel—that you're still a heel, That's the curse of an aching heart.
	(ENSEMBLE CHORUS)
CAST:	She made him what he is today. Let's give three cheers for her.
HOPE:	He done me dirt—the little squirt—he'll spend his life in stir.
BRICE:	It ain't no joke—my heart is broke.
MURPHY:	Don't tear yourself apart—I'll be the Razz Matazz of Alcatraz.
CAST:	That's the curse of an aching heart.
HOPE:	You didn't have to shoot me — you could have killed me with that song!
SOUND:	KNOCK ON DOOR
STAFFORD:	(OFF MIKE…FRENCH ACCENT) Open in the name of the Law.
SOUND:	DOOR OPENS
STAFFORD:	Hello!
BRICE:	Hello, Daddy!
STAFFORD:	Has there been shooting in here?
RAYE:	Yes.
STAFFORD:	Well, you must be more quiet, the neighbours are complaining.
MURPHY:	Wait, Officer, I shot this man because of my love for Fifi…You must take me to prison.
STAFFORD:	Oh…all right.
RAYE:	Wait…Look! The corpse has on a false mustache.
STAFFORD:	I will rip the mustache off.
SOUND:	VERY LONG RIP OF CLOTH

HOPE:	Ouch!—Give me back my upper lip.
STAFFORD:	Voila! It is Gentlemen Joe, the diamond thief…there is fifty thousand francs reward for him.
BRICE:	Oh! I think I'm going to faint…quick, get me a drink of Maxwell House Coffee, good to the last drop.
STAFFORD:	The reward is yours, Charmaine, for discovering him.
RAYE:	Mine…Oh, boy!
MURPHY:	Charmaine, I was only kidding! I never loved anyone but you.
RAYE:	Darling.
BRICE:	Oh, what is to become of me? One of my sweethearts dead and the other has left me…There is only one thing left for me. Oh, Gendarme!
STAFFORD:	Yes, Mademoiselle?
BRICE:	What are you doing tonight?
MUSIC:	(PLAY OFF)
MURPHY:	Thank you, Fanny Brice, Bob Hope, Martha Raye, and Hanley Stafford for a swell "Screen Guild Show."
HOPE:	Oh, George—
MURPHY:	Yes, Bob?
HOPE:	We had a lot of fun tonight, but before we leave I'd like to say for myself and the other members of the cast, that we really enjoyed doing this show. It's not only fun to be on it, but we get a thrill out of helping to achieve the aims of the Motion Picture Relief Fund. Thanks, George, and good night.
MURPHY:	Good night, Bob—And remember, ladies and gentlemen—Next week…same time…same station…the Good Gulf Dealer in your neighborhood joins the Gulf Oil Companies in welcoming you to another Gulf "SCREEN GUILD SHOW" with a drama starring Leslie Howard, Virginia Weidler and _____. Until then, this is George Murphy saying thank you for the Motion Picture Industry and the Gulf Oil Companies. Good night.
MUSIC:	(THEME)

CONTE: We are grateful to MGM for George Murphy, to MGM and the Maxwell House Good News Program for Fanny Brice and Hanley Stafford, and to Paramount and the Pepsodent program for Bob Hope who can be seen in "Never Say Die."

John Conte speaking.

This is the COLUMBIA....BROADCASTING SYSTEM.

Baby Snooks

Hear the Shows...

Buy the Original,

Official Recordings At

www.bickersons.com

PRIVATE EYELASHES

Radio's Lady Detectives

by Jack French

www.privateeyelashes.com

CHECK THESE TITLES! BearManorMedia.com

PO Box 71426 * Albany, GA 31708

Comic Strips and Comic Books of Radio's Golden Age
by Ron Lackmann

From Archie Andrews to Tom Mix, all radio characters and programs that ever stemmed from a comic book or comic strip in radio's golden age are collected here, for the first time, in an easy-to-read, A through Z book by Ron Lackmann!

$19.95   ISBN 1-59393-021-6

Perverse, Adverse and Rottenverse
by June Foray

June Foray, voice of Rocky the Flying Squirrel and Natasha on Rocky and Bullwinkle, has assembled a hilarious collection of humorous essays aimed at knocking the hats off conventions and conventional sayings. Her highly literate work is reminiscent of John Lennon, S.J. Pearlman, with a smattering of P.G. Wodehouse's love of language. This is the first book from the voice of Warner Brothers' Grandma (Tweety cartoons) and Stan Freberg's favorite gal!

$14.95   ISBN 1-59393-020-8

The Old-Time Radio Trivia Book
by Mel Simons

Test your OTR knowledge with the ultimate radio trivia book, compiled by long-time radio personality & interviewer, Mel Simons. The book is liberally illustrated with photos of radio stars from the author's personal collection.

$14.95   ISBN 1-59393-022-4

The Writings of Paul Frees

A full-length screenplay (The Demon from Dimension X!), TV treatments and songs written for Spike Jones—never before published rarities. First 500 copies come with a free CD of unreleased Frees goodies!

$19.95   ISBN 1-59393-011-9

How Underdog Was Born
by creators Buck Biggers & Chet Stover

The creators of Total Television, the brains behind Underdog, Tennessee Tuxedo and many classic cartoons, reveal the origin of one of cartoon's greatest champions—Underdog! From conception to worldwide megahit, the entire story of the birth of Total Television at last closes an important gap in animated television history.

$19.95   ISBN 1-59393-025-9

Daws Butler – Characters Actor
by Ben Ohmart and Joe Bevilacqua

The official biography of the voice of Yogi Bear, Huckleberry Hound and all things Hanna-Barbera. This first book on master voice actor Daws Butler has been assembled through personal scrapbooks, letters and intimate interviews with family and co-workers. Foreword by Daws' most famous student, Nancy Cartwright (the voice of Bart Simpson).

$24.95   ISBN 1-59393-015-1

For these books and more, visit www.bearmanormedia.com
Visa & Mastercard accepted. Add $5.00 postage per book.

BearManorMedia

PO Box 71426 * Albany, GA 31708

Plain Beautiful:
The Life of Peggy Ann Garner

The life story of one of Hollywood's most beloved child actors, whose performance in *A Tree Grows in Brooklyn* won her the Oscar.

$19.95   ISBN 1-59393-017-8

Spotlights & Shadows
The Albert Salmi Story

You know the face. You know the credit list: *Lost in Space, Escape from the Planet of the Apes, Gunsmoke, Bonanza, Kung Fu, The Twilight Zone* and hundreds more...But who was Albert Salmi?

Sandra Grabman's biography is a frank and loving tribute, combined with many memories from Salmi's family, friends, and co-stars, and includes never-before-published memoirs from the man himself. From humble beginnings—to a highly successful acting career—to a tragic death that shocked the world—Albert Salmi's story is unlike any other you'll ever read.

$19.95   ISBN: 1-59393-001-1

For these books and more, visit www.bearmanormedia.com
Visa & Mastercard accepted. Add $5.00 postage per book.

www.ingramcontent.com/pod-product-compliance
Lightning Source LLC
Chambersburg PA
CBHW071438150426
43191CB00008B/1170